GREENWICH PUBS

DAVID C. RAMZAN

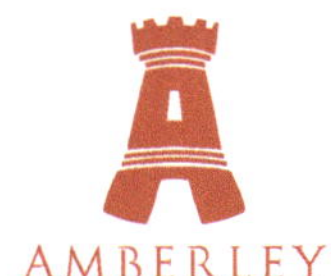

AMBERLEY

I dedicate this publication to all my ancestors, my family and friends who, for over many years past, frequented the pubs of Greenwich, those pubs long gone, and those still serving pints, wines and spirits today, along with cocktails of course.

First published 2023

Amberley Publishing
The Hill, Stroud
Gloucestershire, GL5 4EP

www.amberley-books.com

ISBN 978 1 3981 1560 6 (print)
ISBN 978 1 3981 1561 3 (ebook)

Typesetting by SJmagic DESIGN SERVICES, India.
Printed in the UK.

Appointed GPSR EU Representative: Easy Access
System Europe Oü, 16879218
Address: Mustamäe tee 50, 10621, Tallinn, Estonia
Contact Details: gpsr.requests@easproject.com,
+358 40 500 3575

Contents

	Map	4
	Key	5
	Introduction	6
1	Brewers, Beer and Locals	8
2	Near the River Thames	17
3	West Greenwich	38
4	East Greenwich	66
	Epilogue – The Future of Greenwich Pubs	91
	Bibliography	94
	Notes	94
	Acknowledgements	95
	About the Author	96

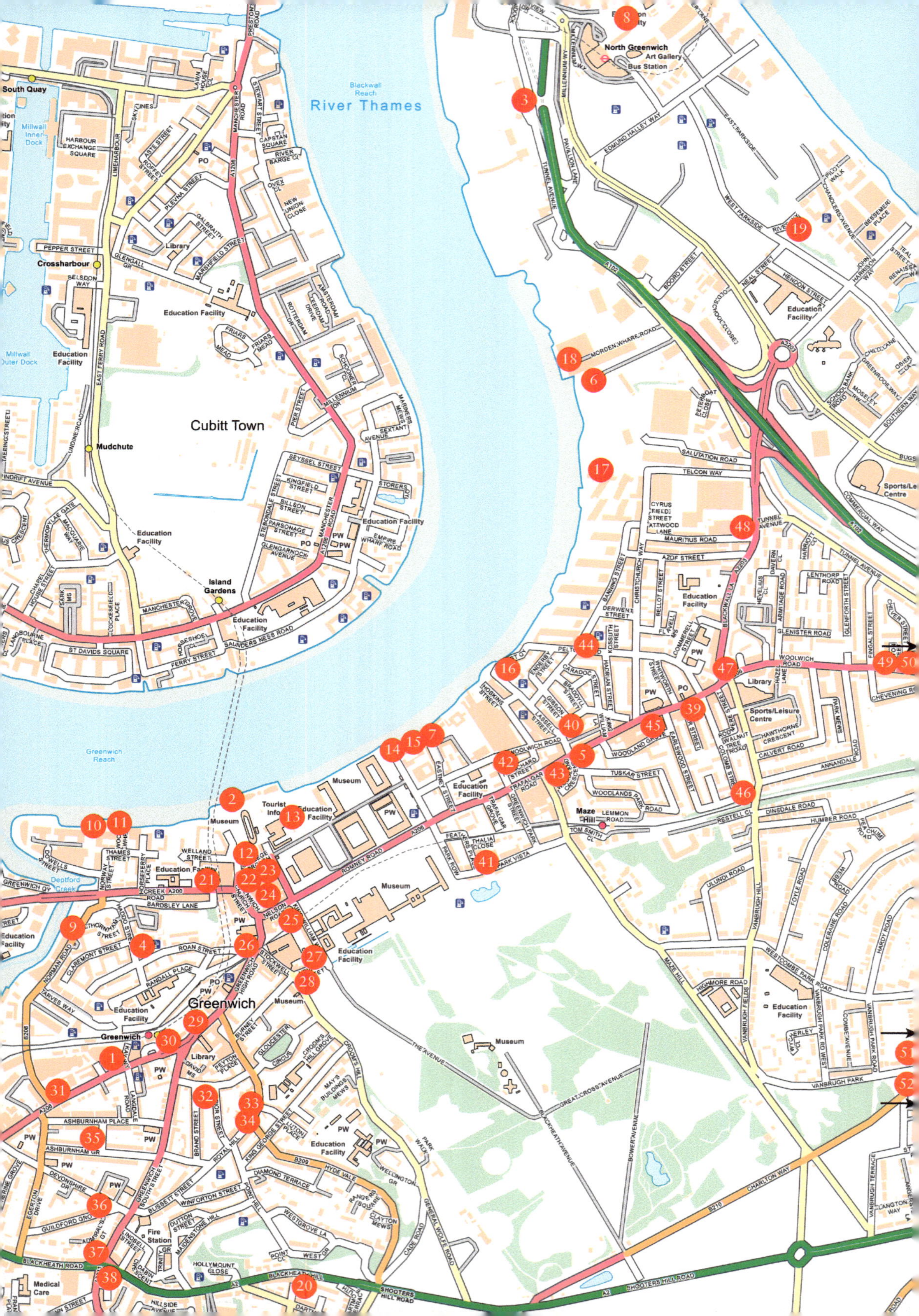

River Thames
Blackwall Reach
South Quay
Millwall Inner Dock
Millwall Outer Dock
Crossharbour
Cubitt Town
Mudchute
Island Gardens
Greenwich Reach
Deptford Creek
Greenwich
North Greenwich
North Greenwich Bus Station
Art Gallery
Maze Hill
Education Facility
Tourist Info
Museum
Library
Sports/Leisure Centre
Medical Care
Fire Station
PEPPER STREET
MANCHESTER ROAD
PRESTONS ROAD
MANCHESTER GROVE
SAUNDERS NESS ROAD
FERRY STREET
ROMNEY ROAD
WOOLWICH ROAD
TRAFALGAR ROAD
SHOOTERS HILL ROAD
BLACKHEATH ROAD
CHARLTON WAY
MORDEN WHARF ROAD
SALUTATION ROAD
TUNNEL AVENUE
EDMUND HALLEY WAY
WEST PARKSIDE
VANBRUGH PARK
MILLENNIUM WAY
ASHBURNHAM PLACE
GUILDFORD GROVE

Key

1. Lovibonds Brewery/Davy's Wine Vaults
2. The Ship Tavern
3. The Star of the East
4. The Bell
5. The Victoria
6. The Sea Witch
7. The Three Crowns
8. London in the Sky
9. The Old Joinery
10. The Oystercatcher
11. The Sail Loft
12. The Gipsy Moth
13. The Old Brewery
14. The Trafalgar Tavern
15. The Yacht
16. The Cutty Sark
17. Enderby House
18. Morden Wharf Terrace
19. The Pilot
20. The Green Man
21. The Gate Clock
22. The Spanish Galleon
23. The Admiral Hardy
24. The Coach & Horses
25. The Kings Arms
26. The Mitre
27. The Greenwich Tavern
28. Ye Olde Rose & Crown
29. The Lost Hour
30. Belushi's
31. The North Pole
32. The Morden Arms
33. Richard I
34. The Prince of Greenwich
35. The Ashburnham Arms
36. The Guildford Arms
37. The Graduate
38. The George & Dragon
39. The British Queen
40. The Duke of Wellington
41. The Plume of Feathers
42. The Star of Greenwich
43. Hardy's
44. The Pelton Arms
45. The Crown
46. The Vanbrugh Tavern
47. Thai Tiger
48. Meantime
49. The River Ale House
50. The Angerstein Hotel
51. The Green Goddess
52. The Royal Standard

Introduction

Between the mid-nineteenth and mid-twentieth century, there were approximately 190 public houses, inns, taverns, beerhouses, and taprooms operating throughout Greenwich parish, with names including Baker and Basket, Black Jack and Shovel, Lampern Dogger, Old Torbay, Ship and Last, and Unicorn, as well as at least four named Red Lion, pubs names no longer remembered by people residing in Greenwich today.

Within the old Greenwich parish boundary there are now fewer than forty pubs, bars, and microbars currently open. The parish boundary is bordered to the west by a Thames tributary, the River Ravensbourne, the boundary running east along the Thames, encompassing Greenwich Marsh, before bearing southwards to meet with the Old Dover Road, then onwards, west, down Blackheath Hill to connect with the Ravensbourne once more. These existing pubs serving refreshments to customers today include one of the earliest, the seventeenth-century Plume of Feathers, to one of the very latest, The Green Goddess, which occupies a converted bank building.

Although the Royal Borough of Greenwich now stretches out to encompass seventeen wards, from Abbey Wood in the east to Mottingham in the south and Creekside to the west, it is the pubs within the old parish boundary which feature in this publication.

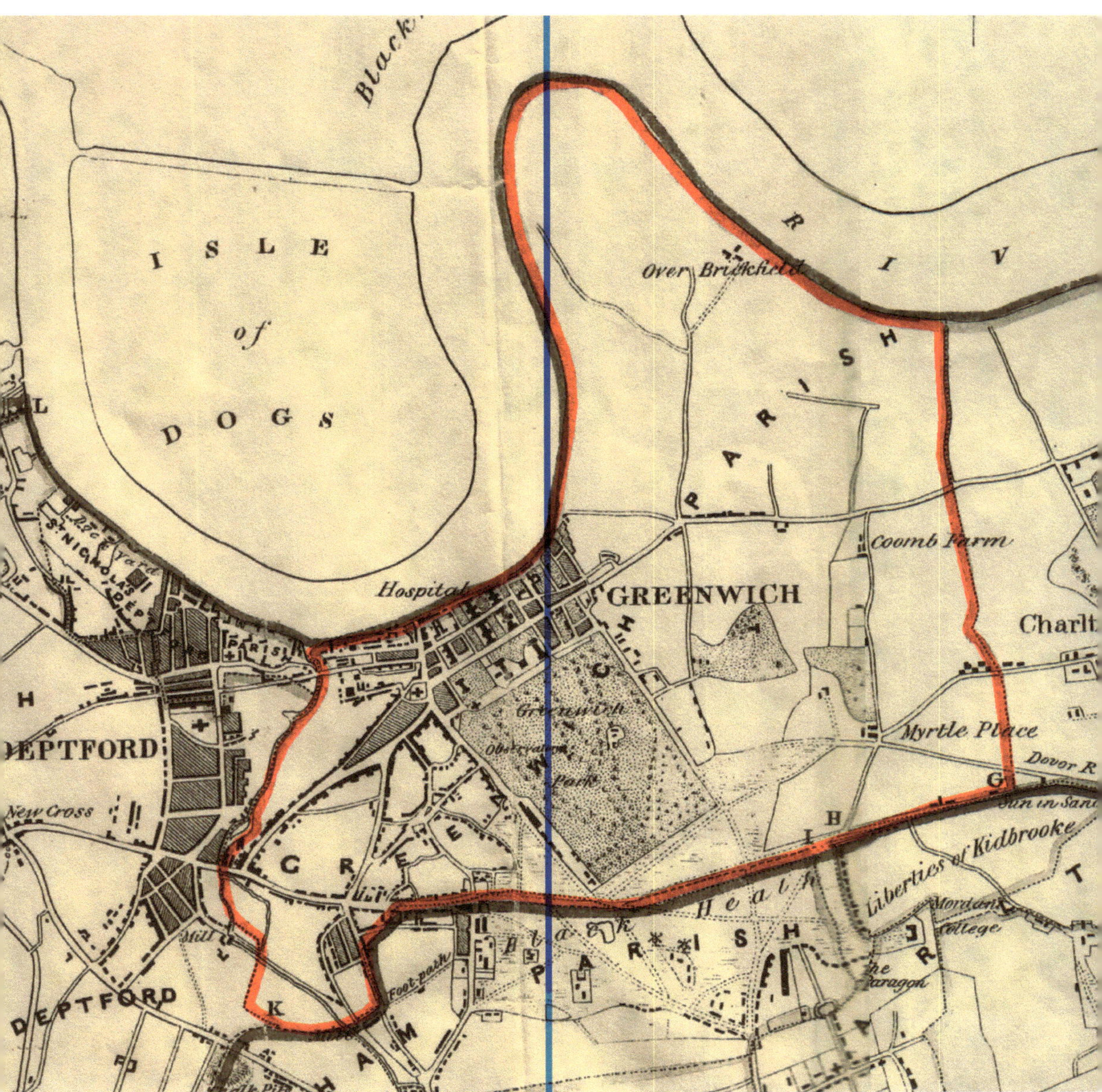

Mid-eighteenth-century map of Greenwich showing the Meridian Line (blue) and parish boundary (red).

I

Brewers, Beer and Locals

Brewing at Greenwich has a deep-rooted history going as far back as early Saxon times, when the manor belonged to the Abbey of Saint Peter of Ghent. Medieval monasteries were important centres of brewing, the friars most likely brewing in the Flemish tradition, using hops rather than brewing conventional unhopped Saxon ale. This was a period when beer was drunk in preference to water drawn up from communal wells, one situated at Stockwell Street West, Greenwich, the well water often tainted and containing life threatening bacteria, the process of brewing killing off many of the microorganisms in water which caused illness or even death.

The Greyfriars of Greenwich, established in 1485, founded a brewhouse in what became the grounds of Henry VII's Greenwich Palace, overlooking the Thames to the west of the Meridian Line, where the tradition of brewing was carried forward at the site through Tudor and Elizabethan times and into the Jacobean period. When Greenwich Palace was abandoned by the monarchy during the English Civil War, then occupied by the Parliamentarians, brewing came to an end. Living under a Puritan regime, the population was discouraged from an over excess of celebrations, which of course included drinking lots of beer, especially during festivals and at Christmas time. Not only did Lord Protector Oliver Cromwell withdraw or refuse licenses of many inns and taverns, but he also sent troops out onto the streets at Christmas to search out those over celebrating with an excess of food and drink, an act of governance unthinkable today, probably?

After the Restoration of the crown in 1660, many drinking establishments and hostelries gradually re-emerged on the highways, byways and lanes running throughout Greenwich parish, and particularly along the waterfront at a place known as Tavern Row, which ran parallel to the river near Greenwich Pier. The first of these ancient taverns on the row was the Rose, another was the Ship, and at the western end, the Three Tuns.

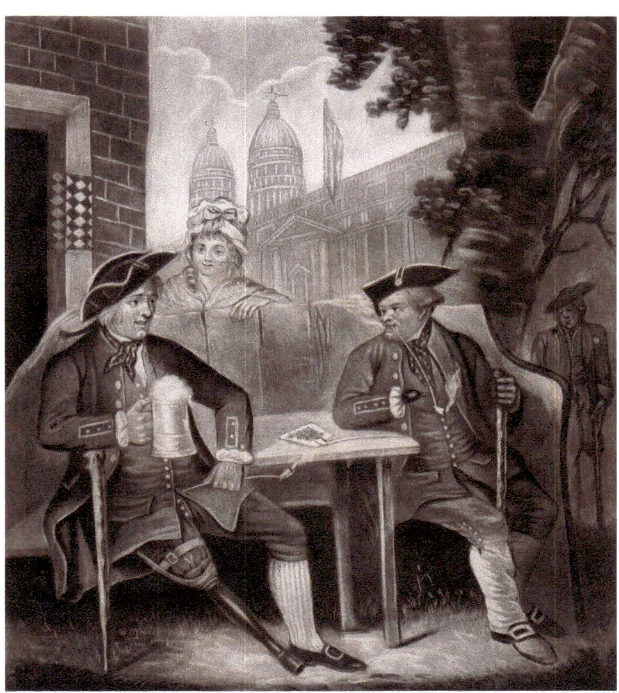

Two Greenwich pensioners sitting in the garden of a tavern, 1791. (Wellcome Collection)

When William and Mary of Orange came to the throne in 1689, Queen Mary founded Greenwich Hospital to support and care for injured and retired Royal Navy seafarers, and a brewhouse was built in 1717 to supply the pensioners with their daily two quarts ration of beer.

The site of the original brewhouse was occupied afterwards by The Old Brewery during the early 2000s, in the Pepys Building of the Old Royal Naval College, where various new beers were brewed and served to thirsty tourists and Greenwich residents.

Through the depravity caused by the overconsumption of gin during the late eighteenth and early nineteenth century, the 1830 Beerhouse Act was introduced liberalising regulations for brewing beer, with the intention of encouraging beer drinking as an alternative to consuming gin, the legislation increasing the number of breweries and brewhouses in Greenwich.

During the early Victorian and late Edwardian periods, when large numbers of workers and their families began moving to the parish to take up the numerous employment opportunities created through the expanding manufacturing, maritime and riverside trades and industries, public houses were built at the end of rows of terraced houses and on the corner of blocks of dwellings erected to accommodate this arrival of new residents. The local pub not only provided beer for thirsty labourers and tradesmen at the end of the working day, they were places where people would socialise and engage with others in their immediate community, many pubs also providing a selection of simple food dishes along with beer, and some offering accommodation as well as entertainment.

Many of these new pubs were built to incorporate architectural features to set them apart from the houses in their vicinity, which resulted in existing taverns, coaching inns, and beerhouses, adding similar features to make them stand out from the competition. Although the earliest hostelries carried traditional names such as Red Lion, Coach and Horses, Fox and Hounds, and White Hart, many new built pubs were named after illustrious and celebrated historic military and industry figures and dignitaries associated with Greenwich, or prominent and significant historical events.

While many of the early alehouses and inns brewed beer on the premises, several breweries were established to supply beer to the increasing number of public houses in the parish, after which there was a clear divide between alehouses brewing their own beer and public houses buying beer from breweries. Powis' Brewery at the site of Greenwich Market, Norfolk and Gloucester Breweries located near Deptford Bridge were prominent brewers at the time. The largest in Greenwich parish was Lovibonds, located on Greenwich Road, now Greenwich High Road.

Lovibonds originated in the West Country before opening a brewery at a Deptford pub, the Nag's Head, then relocating to a purpose-built brewery on Greenwich High Road, the land purchased from the London & Greenwich Railway. Damaged by bombing during the Second World War, Lovibonds was soon back up and running, supplying beer to local pubs and the population of Greenwich once again. After repairs were carried out to the buildings, Lovibonds continued in operation well into the late 1960s, when the premises were closed and sold to John Davy & Co., wine merchants. The old brewery buildings are now known as Davy's Wine Vaults, comprising of bars, dining areas, an outdoor terrace and wine shop.

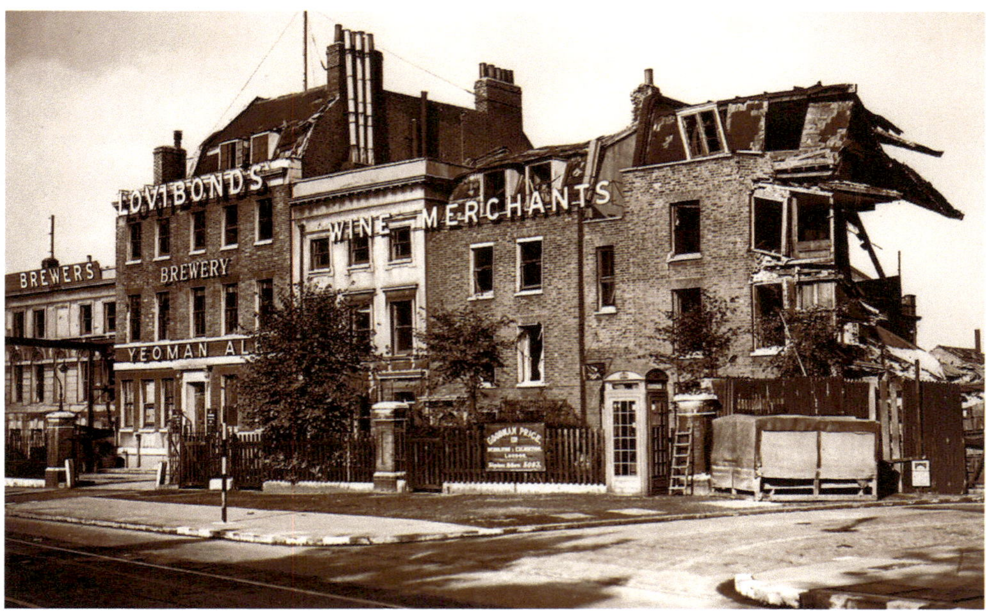

Lovibonds Brewery after being damaged by bombing during the Second World War.

To the rear, the yard, where barrels and bottles of beer were once loaded onto to carts for distribution throughout Greenwich and the south-east of London, has been transformed into a large undercover outdoor seating area where there are various historical artifacts on display connected to the wine industry. From the days when the brewery was once at the centre of the Greenwich community, Davy's Wine Vaults continues to embrace the local community spirit by holding a variety of events including classic car shows, comedy nights, film nights and festive seasonal celebrations at the old brewery buildings.

The rise of the brewing industry resulted in an increase of associated local crafts and trades such as maltsters, bottle makers, millers, coopers and draymen, the produce to make beer, the hops and grains, transported to the breweries and maltsters up river by barge, or by road on carts, and then by freight train.

By the early 1900s, national breweries had purchased many independent small breweries and had taken over ownership of a majority of local public houses, operated under a pub tenancy agreement or tied lease, which typically included a beer tie where a specified quantity of spirits and beers had to be purchase through the holding brewery or a named supplier, instead of managed as a free house where a publican bought stock as and where they wanted.[1]

Divided into east and west by the Meridian Line, established in 1884 as Zero Degrees Longitude to serve as a reference point for astronomical observations, navigation, and

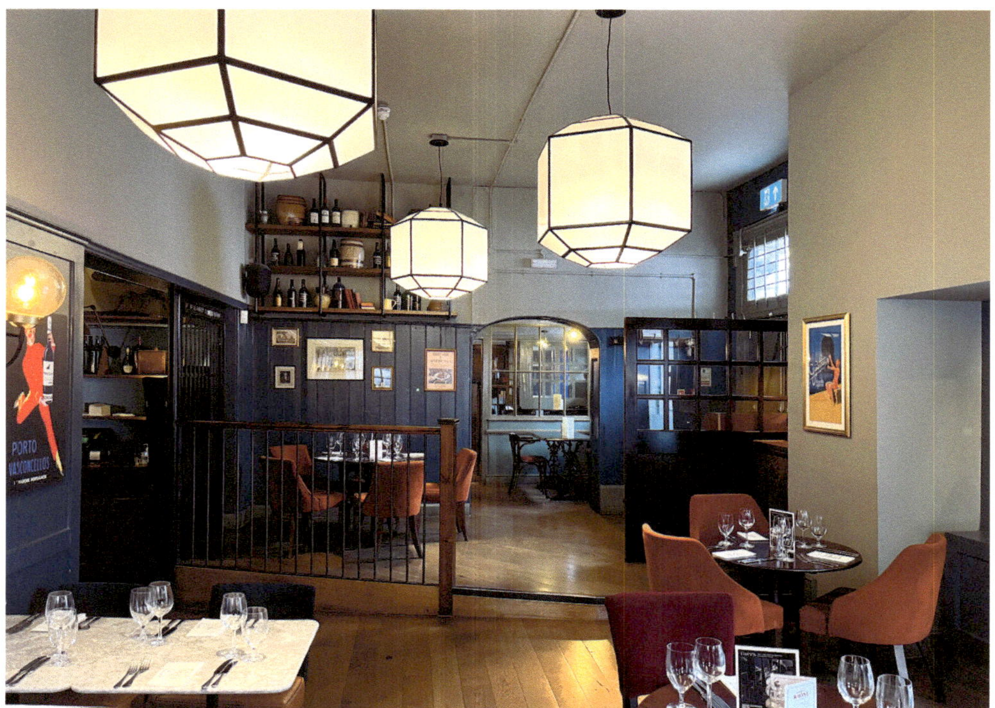

Davy's Wine Vaults dining area, 2022.

zonal timing, the parish comprised of upper-class and working-class communities. The large spacious mansions and elegant houses of merchants and industrialists occupied areas of land to the west and south of Greenwich, while a majority of working-class families resided in terraced properties to the east, and northward towards Greenwich Marsh, areas each side of the Meridian Line abundant with a variety of taverns, coaching inns, alehouses, and beerhouses.

Along the south bank of the Thames, where mercantile and industrial trades flourished each side of the seventeenth-century Greenwich Hospital, there were a number of riverside pubs nestling between warehouse buildings, yards, and wharfs, and as industry evolved across Greenwich Marsh, beerhouses and pubs could be found located amongst the many houses of the industrial workforce, as well as alongside commercial sites and boat yards.

Usually the pub would have a selection of bars where you could choose to drink, dependent on your attire and your status in the community: a saloon or lounge for when dressed in your finery; a public bar, usually for working classes; a snug, a small more private area with access to the counter, and occasionally an off-sales, where you could purchase beer to drink at home.

The pub provided a meeting place for local residents and became a focus of their community, as indispensable as their church or local grocery store. Pubs also offered various forms of entertainment, such as music and a good old sing-song, while snooker, bar billiards, dominoes, cards, and darts became popular games played by the locals. One time resident of Greenwich, Henry VIII was a keen dart player, where it was said the king outstripped everyone he played against. In 1532, Anne Boleyn presented her prospective husband with his own set of darts. Greenwich-born Henry also played football too, a sport that many young men took part in from the late 1800s onwards by forming teams based at their local pub, its regulars also forming rugby and cricket teams, the pub landlord often sponsoring the team where a motley body of players would run out with the name of the pub emblazoned across their shirts.

For many years Greenwich pubs have been a focal point for members of my family and friends, gathering together for Sunday lunchtime drinks, weekend nights out, various celebratory occasions or just a quick beer after work.

Our local pubs also offered casual working opportunities too, either serving behind the bar, or waiting table at pubs offering food. Before the Second World War, my grandfather Charlie would bring in some extra cash on a Sunday by going round the local pubs raffling a rabbit for lunch, which would then be won by his brother-in-law, Alf, who just so happened to be in the pub at the same time!

One of my first part-time jobs, when just turning eighteen, was serving behind the bar of the Pilot on Greenwich Marsh, and later at the British Queen, now a turf accountants on Woolwich Road. Many of my friends also took a turn serving behind the bar at several of our locals, as well as a majority of us playing in a pub darts team or football team.

As years passed by, many well established Greenwich pubs were lost during the latter half of the twentieth century, demolished after damaged through bombing of the Second World War, or knocked down to make way for regeneration projects of the mid-1900s.

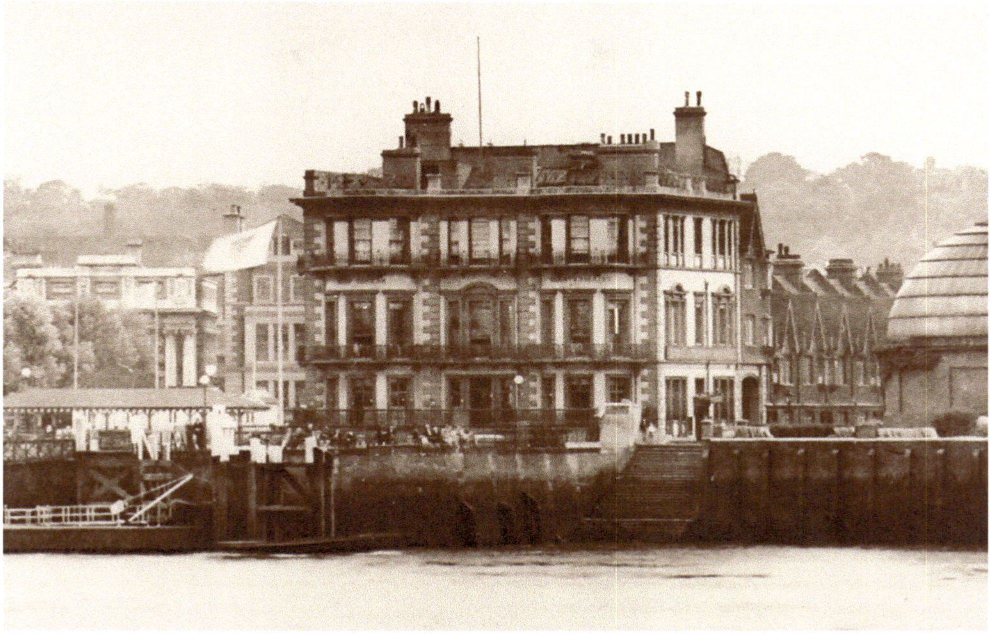

The Ship Tavern, Greenwich riverfront, early 1900s.

The Ship Tavern adjacent to Greenwich Pier was one of Greenwich's most famous riverside pubs, frequented by writers, actors and Members of Parliament travelling down from central London by riverboat to dine on whitebait dinners, the little silver fish caught by Peter boats fishing on the Thames. One of many pubs suffering from bomb damage, the Ship Tavern was pulled down after the Second World War, and a dry dock built near the site to accommodate the clipper ship *Cutty Sark*.

However, many of Greenwich's pubs were saved from demolition by repurposing and conversion for residential and commercial use. The Duke of Wellington on Old Woolwich Road was converted into flats, as was the Man in the Moon further to the west of this ancient thoroughfare. The William IV, on Trafalgar Road, reverted to its original purpose of a hotel, with a Turkish restaurant on the ground floor, changing its name to Ye Olde Turk, then becoming a Vietnamese restaurant, the Tam Viet, before its closure in 2021.

The Star of the East on Greenwich Marsh, adjacent to Blackwall Tunnel entrance, is now a motor spare parts shop, the building currently under negotiations for its sale, and the Bell near Creek Bridge has been converted into a Turkish café.

Walking the streets and lanes of the present-day Greenwich parish, you will come across various buildings recognisable as a one-time public house, a few identified by the title of the pub, or an emblem of the brewery, displayed high up above an entrance fronted by large wooden double doors. On other buildings there may still be faded painted words or signage on an outer wall, or large windows with panes of decoratively etched opaque glass, which gives identification that this building was once a public house.

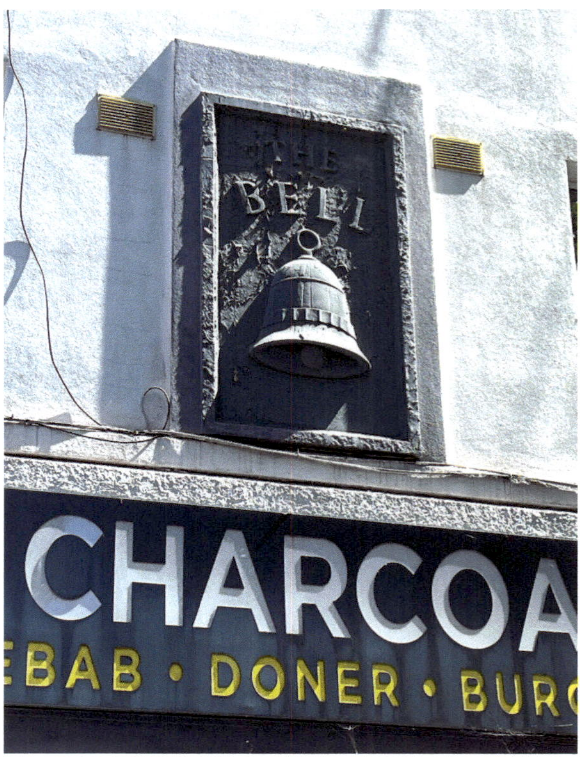

The Bell pub sign on the upper part of the former pub building, Haddo Street.

Other well-established boozers, however, fared less well. The popular British Sailor, situated close to the river on Lassell Street, run by licensees Eddie and Linda Farmer, where many of Greenwich's younger locals would meet up for fun music nights during weekends of the eighties, was sold to developers when under new management, and then knocked down to build apartments in 2001.

The Victoria on Trafalgar Road, another proper boozer where my friends and I were also regulars up until it's closure when licensee Dave Buckingham moved on, was also sold off and then demolished to make way for an apartment block erected on the corner plot.

On Greenwich Marsh the Sea Witch, situated on the riverside, which dated to the mid-1800s, received a direct hit during the Blitz, while the Mitre Arms, built in the late 1800s and located adjacent to Blackwall Tunnel entrance, survived the bombing raids to become a popular music venue in the mid-1900s, and then a nightclub. The pub was subsequently demolished and replaced by Studio 338, an Ibiza-style mega-club playing electronic sounds, a fashionable place to go for students and a younger set of clientele.

Through the late twentieth century and leading up the second millennium, a gradual rise in leisure activities, home entertainment and off-licence outlets selling alcoholic beverages cheaper than could be purchased in public houses, along with a changing social life, brought about an economic downturn in the pub industry, where it was estimated that between 2002 and 2017, a quarter of London's pubs had closed.[2]

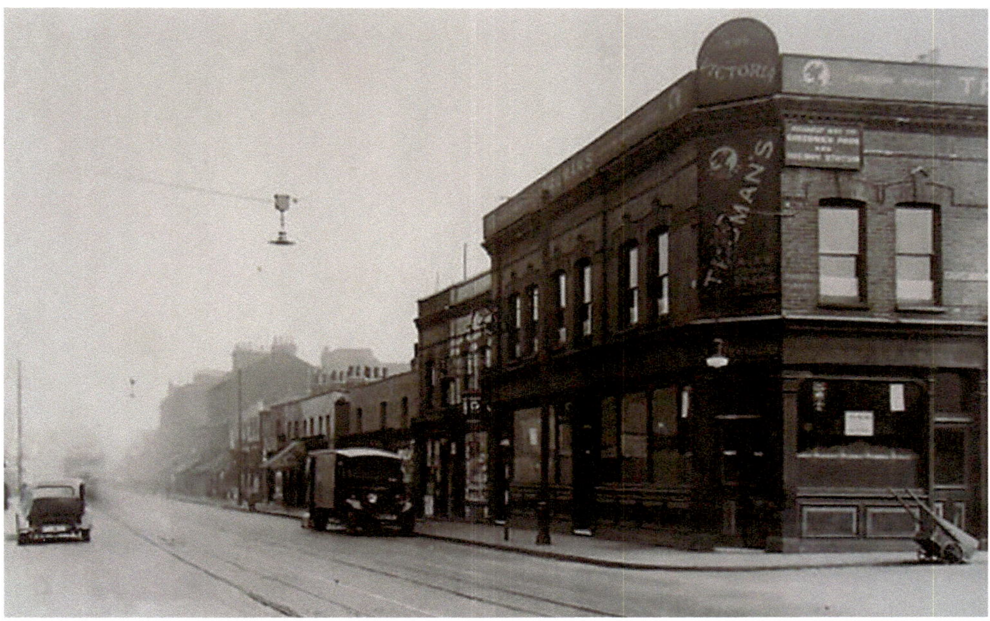

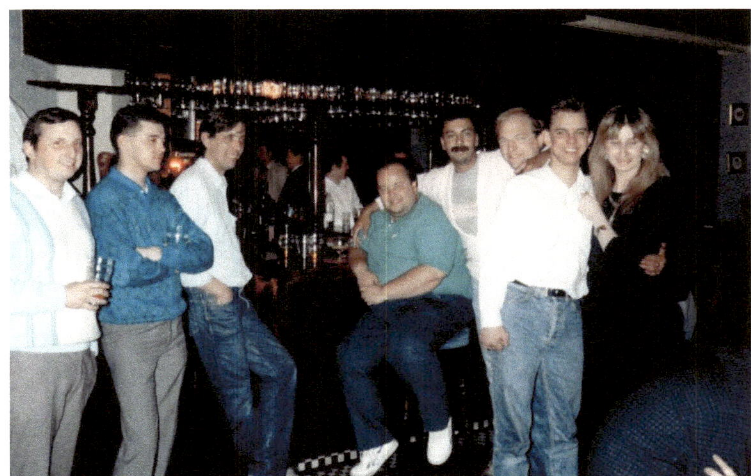

Above: The Victoria, Trafalgar Road, late 1800s.

Right: The author, fourth from right, and locals of the Victoria, late 1980s.

This trend was reflected within Greenwich parish boundary, as all areas came under comprehensive residential and light industrial redevelopment with little consideration for what pubs meant to the local community. Many of the once well-established hostelries were either demolished to make way for these new developments or converted for other uses. The closure of local pubs frequently resulted in the disappearance of various associated social activities, communal events, and sports clubs.

The latest pub to fall under the developers' hammer was the Thames, formerly the Rose & Crown, located on Thames Street, West Greenwich. Although the notable free house had served the local community of riverside workers and residents since the 1830s, the pub, said to have been haunted by an ex-docker, closed in the late 1990s, as new buildings rose all around. After various parties made attempts to have the old boozer restored to its former glory, the council, without discussion, approved its demolition and the pub, the last remaining Victorian building in that historic area of Greenwich, was demolished in 2021, with very little notice of the pub's destruction, and replaced by a high block of apartments. The pub's demise followed the demolition of two of its neighbours a few years earlier, the Old Loyal Briton also on Thames Street, and the Lord Hood on Creek Road, both replaced by … more apartments.

A majority of the remaining public houses serving beer to residents and tourists today have been extensively altered over the years, with their decor updated and several going through a succession of name changes. Only a few, however, retain the character and atmosphere of times past.

At one time it was common that a landlord or landlady held the licence to run the pub, and would often live as well as work at the premises. However, in recent years, it is more likely a pub will be run by a general manager, or duty managers, on behalf of an absent landlord, owner, or pub chain.

At the turn of the twenty-first century, with Greenwich at the centre of the millennium celebrations, there came a resurgence of micro and small independent breweries, specialising in providing traditional ales and craft beers brewed on their own premises and served directly to their regulars.

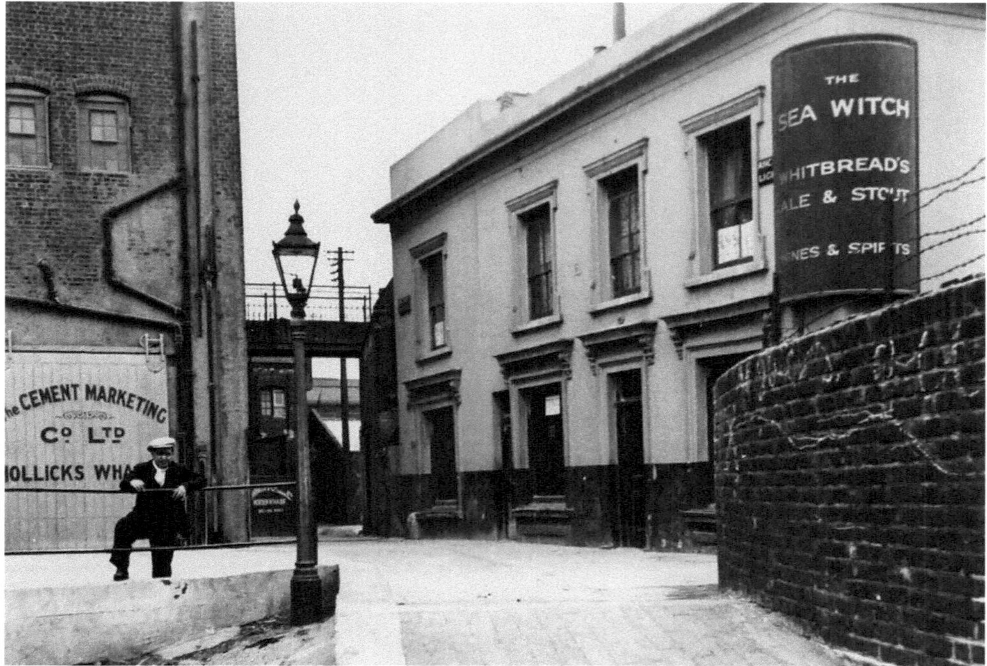

The Sea Witch, demolished after being severely damaged during a bombing raid.

2

Near the River Thames

At the turn of the twentieth century, the riverfront along the south bank of the Thames at Greenwich was a bustling hive of activity, where vessels of all types, shapes and sizes offloaded goods and cargo at the various wharfs and jetties, as well as taking on ballast and aggregates from quays, or coal and coke residue from power stations and gasworks. Larger craft mooring at Greenwich Reach and Blackwall Reach moved their cargo to and from shore by lighter, a capacious flat bottom barge able to carry tons of payload about the river by lightermen using nothing more than long oars up until the introduction of steam tugs.

The watermen and lightermen working on the river, and the personnel attending the Royal Naval College, formerly Greenwich Hospital for seafaring pensioners, frequented the many pubs once situated along the river, from Deptford Creek to Greenwich Marsh.

As work on the Thames and the industries along the river fell into decline, many of Greenwich's riverside pubs lost custom, becoming financially unviable to maintain and run, particularly when the area came under regeneration through the latter part of the 1900s, the land on which they were built becoming a valuable commodity for real estate developers and investors.

Many pubs not destroyed by bombing during the Second World War eventually stopped pouring pints, and closed their doors for good, either demolished to make way for new property developments or converted and refurbished for other uses. Those pubs which remained along the riverside were forced to adapt to survive.

To the north of Greenwich Marsh, a large exhibition centre, the Dome, was erected in the late 1900s, to the east of where the Greenwich Prime Meridian Line passes by, built as the focal point for the second millennium celebrations. On completion of the Dome's Millennium Experience, the huge structure was later converted into a state-of-the-art music, sport, and entertainment venue, the O2, with shops, restaurants, bars, and cafés.

Moving forward into the twenty-first century, Greenwich Marsh underwent a period of regeneration, where much of the industrial vacated land was then secured for the

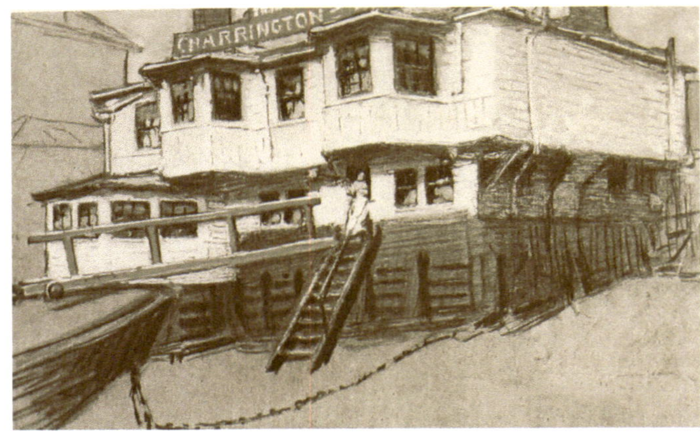

The Three Crowns, High Bridge Wharf, demolished during the 1930s.

building of apartments, hotels, work spaces, restaurants, and a university, along with permanent and temporary pop-up bars, and in February 2023, a new JD Wetherspoon pub, The Stargazer, opened within the O2's Entertainment District, which features a large beer garden with views across the Thames towards Canary Wharf.

Along with these new property developments on the riverfront and areas across Greenwich Marsh, renamed Greenwich Peninsula, there came a new generation of workers and residents, which resulted in the creation of several contemporary

London in the Sky Bar, open during the summer months.

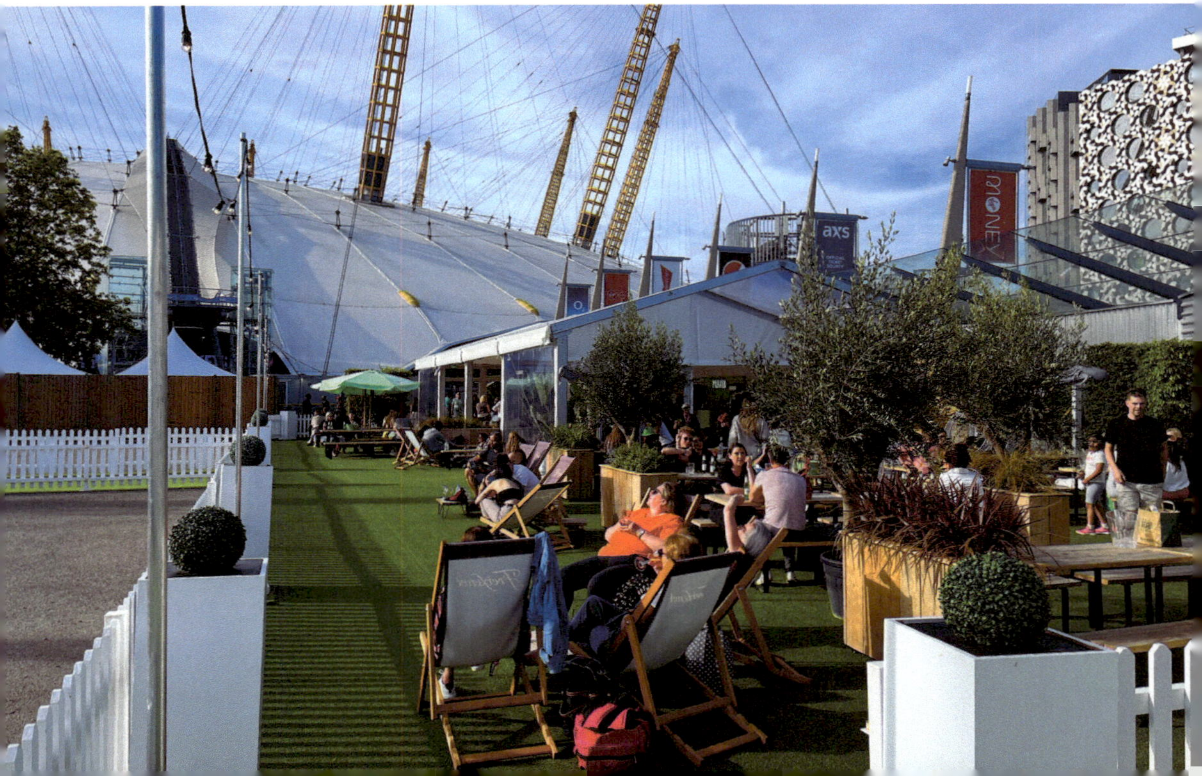

restaurants with bars, and the conversion of historic commercial buildings into modern styled pubs and microbreweries, all in competition with the few remaining old style boozers from years gone by.

THE OLD JOINERY, Ravensbourne Wharf, Norman Road

Overlooking Deptford Creek, a tidal tributary of the River Thames, The Old Joinery occupies a capacious brick-lined warehouse and expansive outside seating area, with bars serving beer and food, and a large entertainment space for live music events. Located to the east of the River Ravensbourne, formerly an area of industry, the warehouse, built towards the late 1800s, occupies the site of Headley Oil Mills, the mills grinding and crushing seeds and vegetables to produce oil for commercial sale during the nineteenth century.

Converted in 2017 into an art studio, film location and event space, The Old Joinery evolved into a bar and eatery, open at weekends, serving wines, spirits, cocktails, locally brewed beers, and street food. Along with regular DJ nights, live music performances take place throughout the year, where musicians such as Paul-Rooney Angel, Errol Linton and Chris Difford of Squeeze have appeared. However, like many previous industrial sites both sides of Deptford Creek, those which remain, including The Old Joinery warehouse, are under constant threat from developers acquiring the land to build more high-rise apartments.

The Old Joinery.

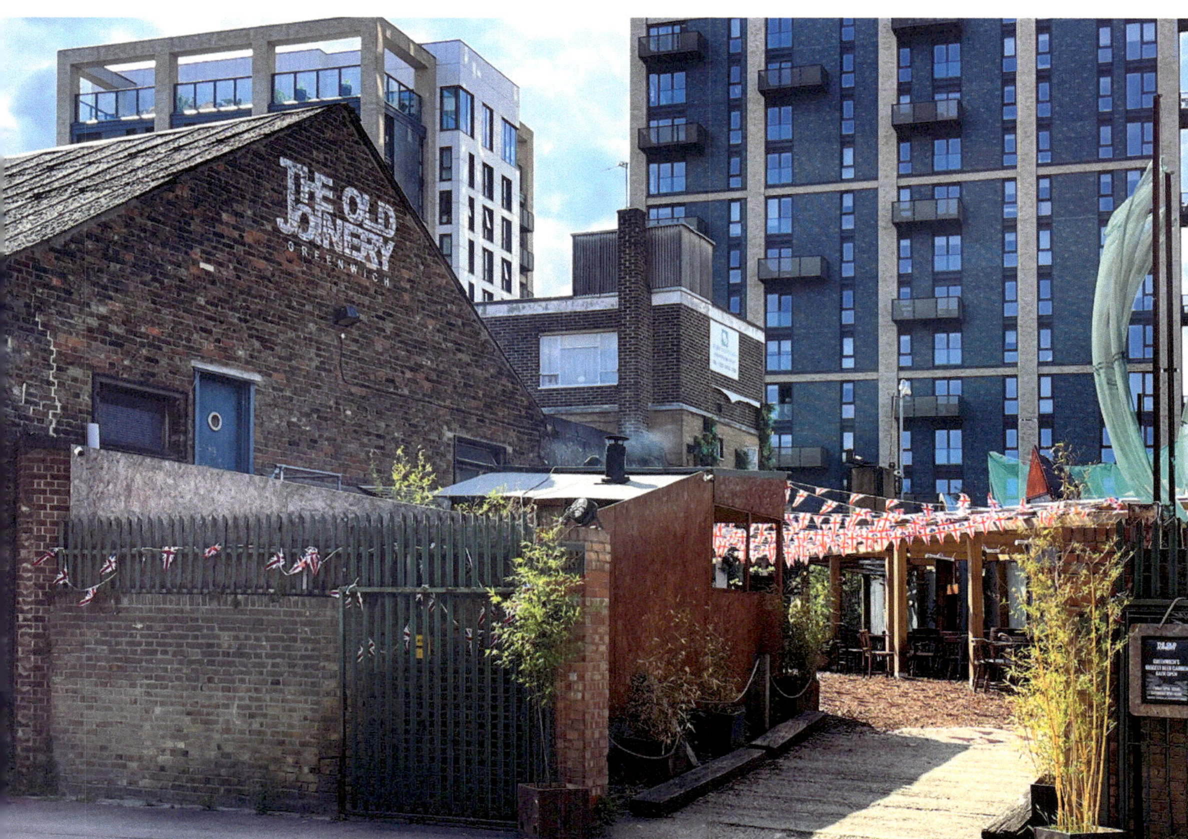

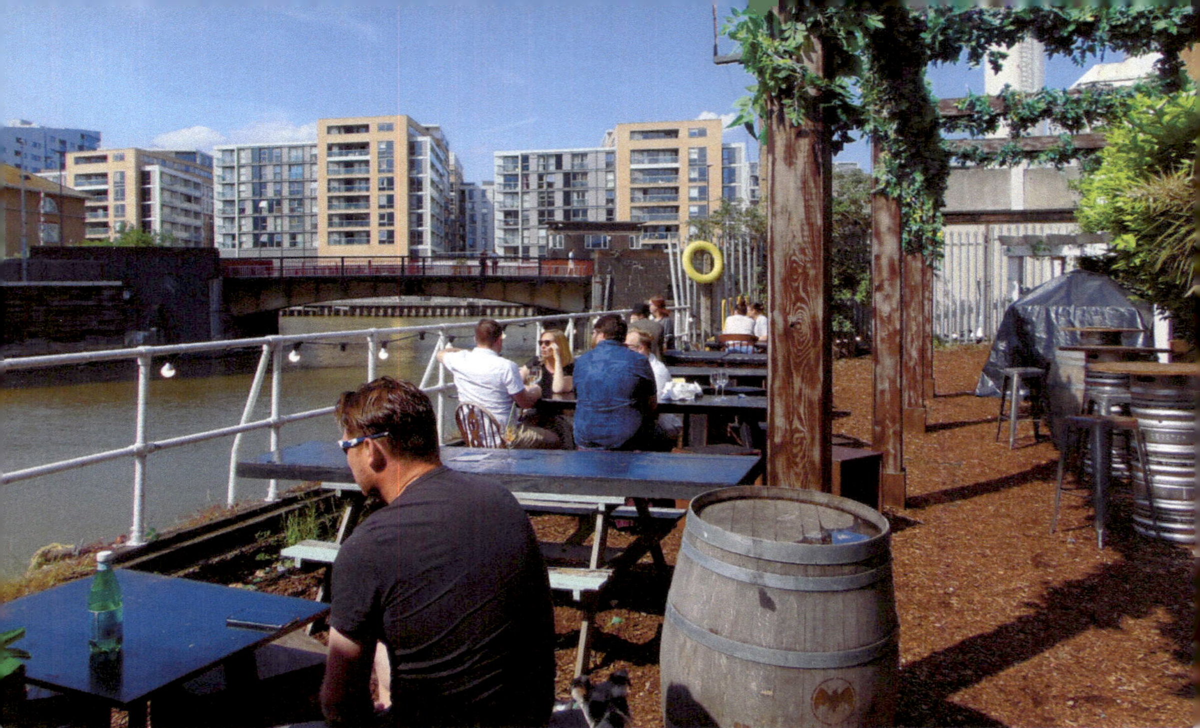

The Old Joinery's riverside beer garden.

THE OYSTERCATCHER, Kings Lodge, Victoria Parade

One of the riverfront's newest pubs, opened in 2019 by the Mosaic Pub Group at the Capital Quay complex, the Oystercatcher is split over two floors at the base of a contemporary six-storey block of apartments and retail units. The modern open plan bar with stylish bright décor and kitchen occupies the ground floor, with a dining area overlooking the Thames situated on the first floor.

Outside, the terrace stretches the length of the building running adjacent to the Thames, with tables and chairs for outside eating and drinking sheltered under wide canopies. The Oystercatcher takes its name from a coastal and estuary wading bird which feeds on various species of shellfish, including oysters, which were once found in abundance along the outer reaches of the Thames, the molluscs becoming a popular cheap source of food for the common people of London during the 1800s.

This very modern drinking establishment's clientele is mostly made up of tourists visiting Greenwich and young upwardly mobile professionals moving into the area to take up residence in the large number of apartments which have been built along this stretch of the river, all within easy access of central London by riverbus and train services.

Before the regeneration of this North West Ward of Greenwich, during the late 1800s and early 1900s, the riverfront consisted of a gasworks, ship and boat yards, an ironworks, a ferry, jetties, and wharfs, including Wood Wharf, now the site of the Oystercatcher. The riverside landscape of modern, tall, glass-fronted buildings, seen by passengers arriving by pleasure boats and fast twin-hulled commuter craft at Greenwich Pier today, is very much different from the mishmash of wood- and brick-built structures and workshops that would have once greeted passengers of paddle steamers in years gone by.

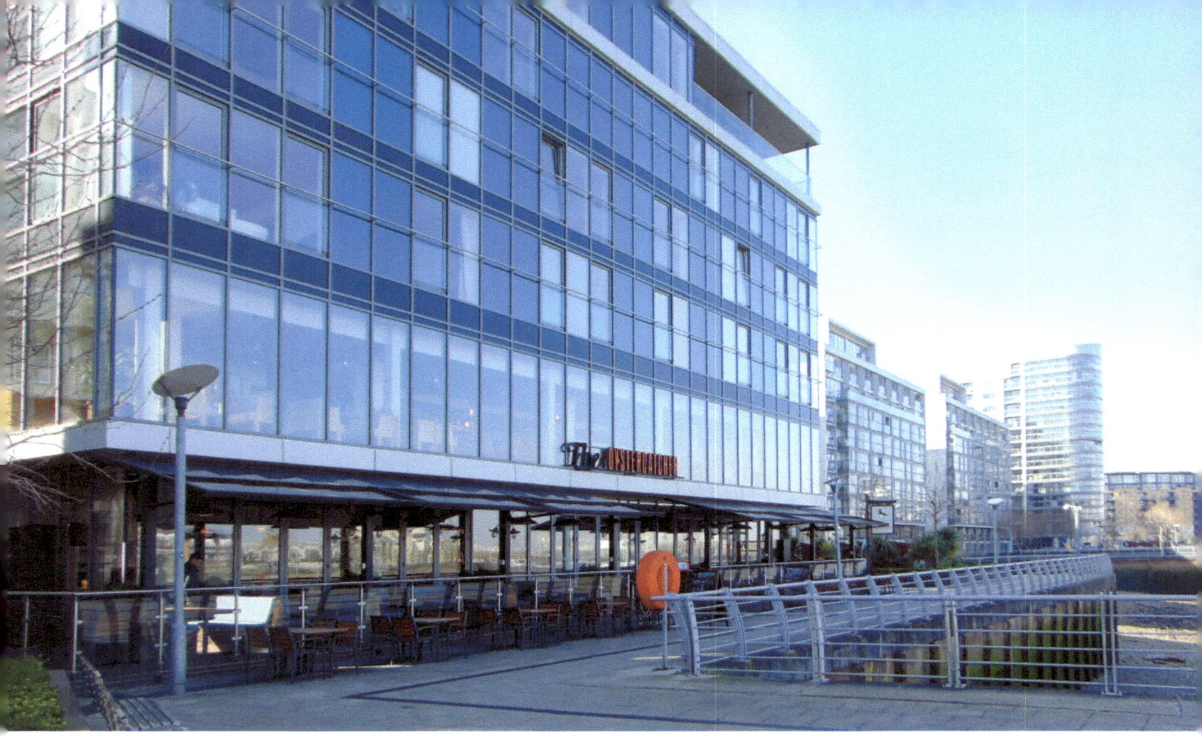

Above: The Oystercatcher riverside.

Below: The Oystercatcher's general manager Tom Rickard and supervisor Paul Moran.

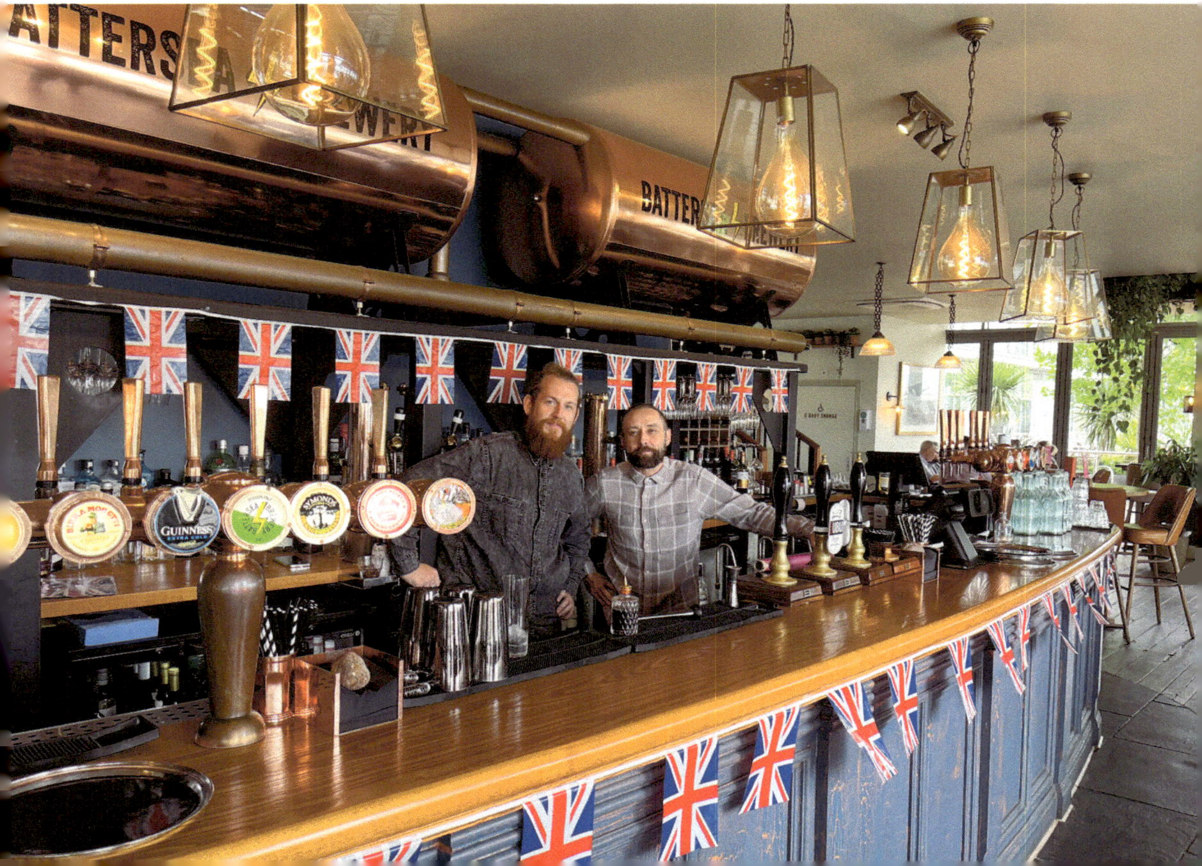

THE SAIL LOFT, Victoria Parade

Positioned further forward on the riverside, to the east of the Oystercatcher, is another bright, spacious open plan pub, the Sail Loft, which opened in 2016. One of a chain of Fullers properties, the Sail Loft also occupies two lower floors of a glass-fronted apartment block. Similar to its neighbouring competitor, the Sail Loft interior is of modern design, with exposed brass ducting, contemporary furniture, wooden fittings and flooring, and an island bar and open view kitchen, all on the ground floor.

Up on the first floor, overlooking the Thames, is another bar, restaurant, and more seating for dining or just having a casual drink while looking out towards the modern high-rise offices and apartments at Canary Wharf opposite, formerly known as the Isle of Dogs. Outside on the ground floor is an undercover seating area, also in view of the river, where you can watch riverboats pass by.

Although it is doubtful the pubs name has any connections with any specific sail loft that occupied a variety of old buildings previously on the site, by its close proximity to the old Billingsgate Dock, once the centre of the Greenwich fishing industry, it is very likely fishing boats would have stored their canvas sheets in sail lofts of workshops in the near vicinity of this modern pub.

The Sail Loft riverside.

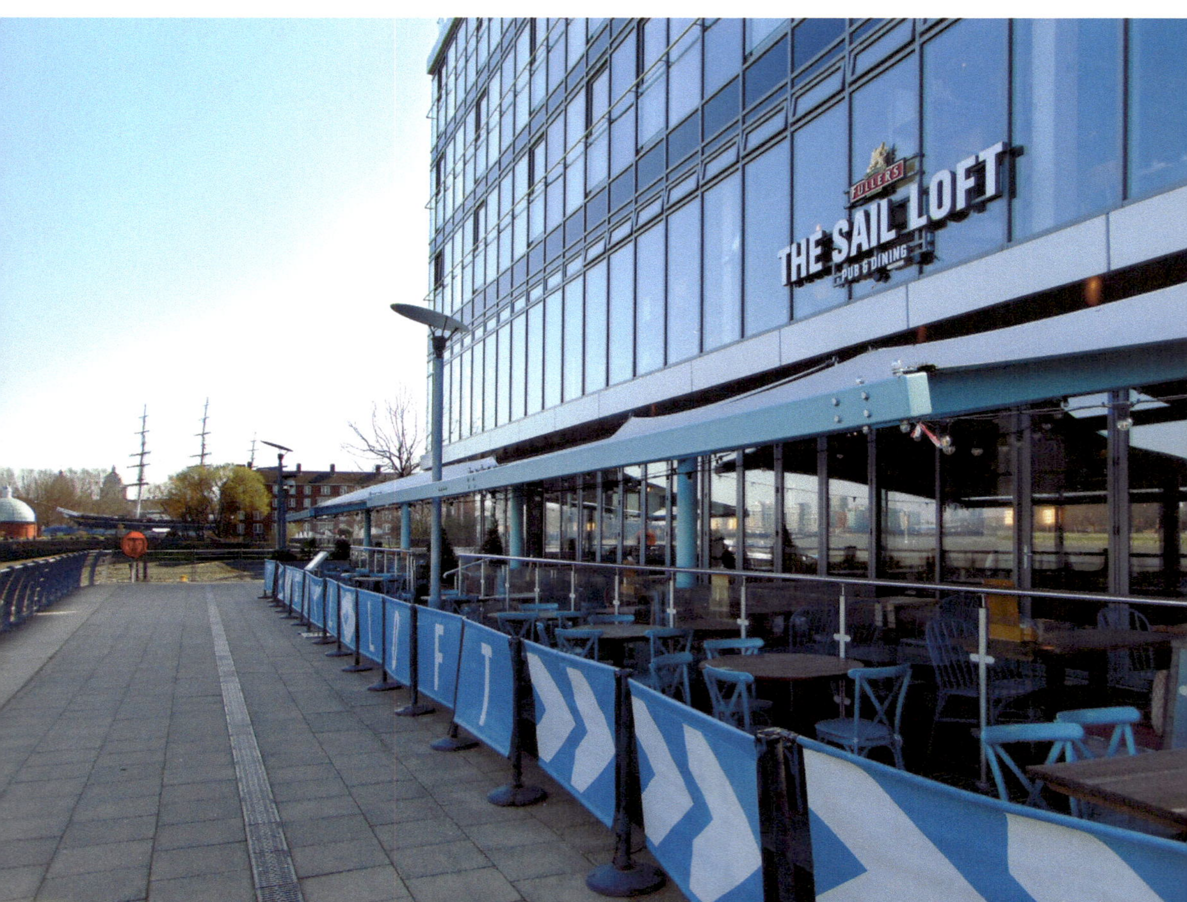

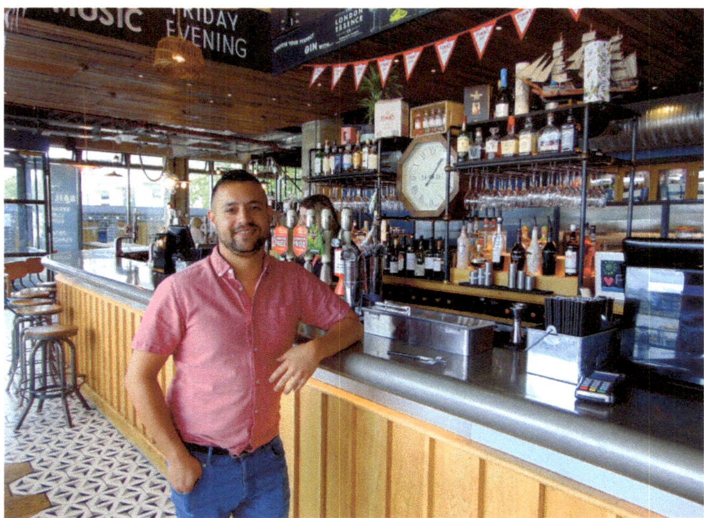

The Sail Loft's deputy manager Milo Taylor.

THE GIPSY MOTH, Greenwich Church Street

One public house close to the River Thames has taken the name of an actual world-famous sailing vessel, the *Gipsy Moth*. Previously named the Wheatsheaf, in 1972, after Sir Francis Chichester was knighted at Greenwich in recognition of the magnificent feat of becoming the first person to sail around the globe single-handed, racing against times set by the old clipper ships, such as the *Cutty Sark*, the pub was renamed after Chichester's ketch, *Gipsy Moth*, which was placed in dry dock on display to the public adjacent to the Greenwich Foot Tunnel.

The pub once stood in the middle of a row of early nineteenth-century terraced houses; however, after bombs fell across the area during the Second World War, the damaged properties to the north were all demolished, including the old Ship Tavern, the Wheatsheaf the last property of a surviving row to the south.

The first recorded publican in 1805, was William Roberts, and like many public houses there would be a succession of licensees and landlords throughout its history, including the Wheatsheaf's first landlady, Mrs Keziah Hall, who took over the pub in 1891 after the death of her husband Edward. It was not unusual for the landlord's widow to take over a pub on her husband's death, but it was highly unlikely a pub would be run by a women on her own if not first married to the landlord.

Pubs named Wheatsheaf were more commonly found in rural areas, usually surrounded by farming communities, and although when built the pub was situated in a riverside working community, Greenwich was then located within the county of Kent, and the pub's name may have been chosen to reflect a time when the riverside settlement was surrounded by fields of wheat, or in recognition of the wheat cargoes transported by Thames barges up river from Kent and Essex farms to the flour mills on the River Ravensbourne close by.

Refurbished since changing its name to the Gipsy Moth, the Grade II listed pub now has several bars and dining areas, a large airy conservatory with gardens to the rear, one giving a grand view of the *Cutty Sark*, the only surviving clipper ship which circumnavigated the globe carrying cargoes of tea and wool in record times.

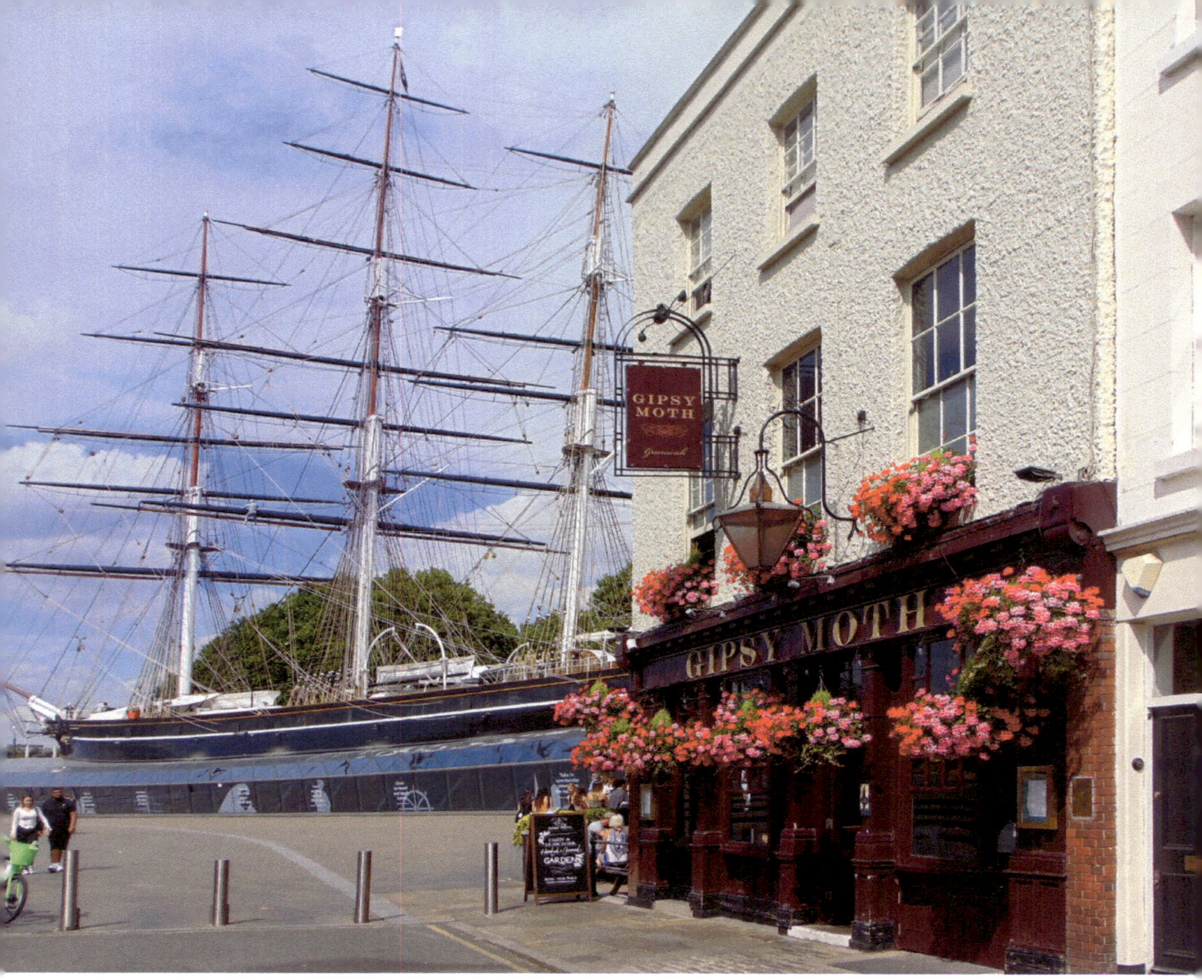

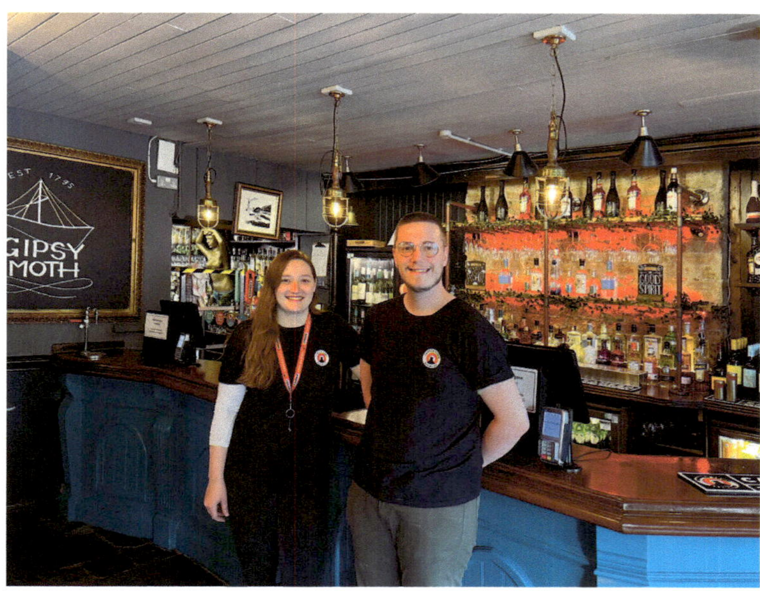

Above: The Gipsy Moth, adjacent to the historic clipper *Cutty Sark*.

Left: The Gipsy Moth's manager Chris White and duty manager Rosie.

THE OLD BREWERY, The Pepys Building, Old Royal Naval College

Situated withing the grounds of the Old Royal Naval College, a World Heritage Site, the Old Brewery was formerly owned by local brewery Meantime and was then taken over in 2017 by the pub chain Youngs. Occupying part of the Grade II Romano-Greco palatial-style Pepys Building, designed by two Royal Engineers, General Clarke and General Pudsey, built towards the latter half of the nineteenth-century, the Old Brewery is situated upon the original site of the Greenwich Hospital brewhouse, where brewing followed a centuries-long tradition at the site. The beer was piped directly to Greenwich Hospital pensioners dining room, the pensioners, injured and retired Royal Naval sailors, were permanent residents of the hospital and enjoyed their rations of beer. Known by locals as Greenwich Geese, the pensioners, recognisable by their long blue frockcoats with gold trim and black tri-corn hats, some pensioners missing a limb or an eye, the result of active service, were a rowdy bunch of fellows who frequented Greenwich's beerhouses and taverns, ready to accept a drink in exchange for a tale about their exploits fighting for king and country on the high seas.

When the pensioners moved out of the hospital in the late 1800s, the buildings were acquired by the Royal Navy for training officers, and although not so rowdy as their predecessors, naval officers often went out drinking in the local pubs. While the Duke of Edinburgh and later Prince Charles attended the Royal Naval College during their respective years serving in the Royal Navy, both were often seen out having a beer in pubs close to the college.

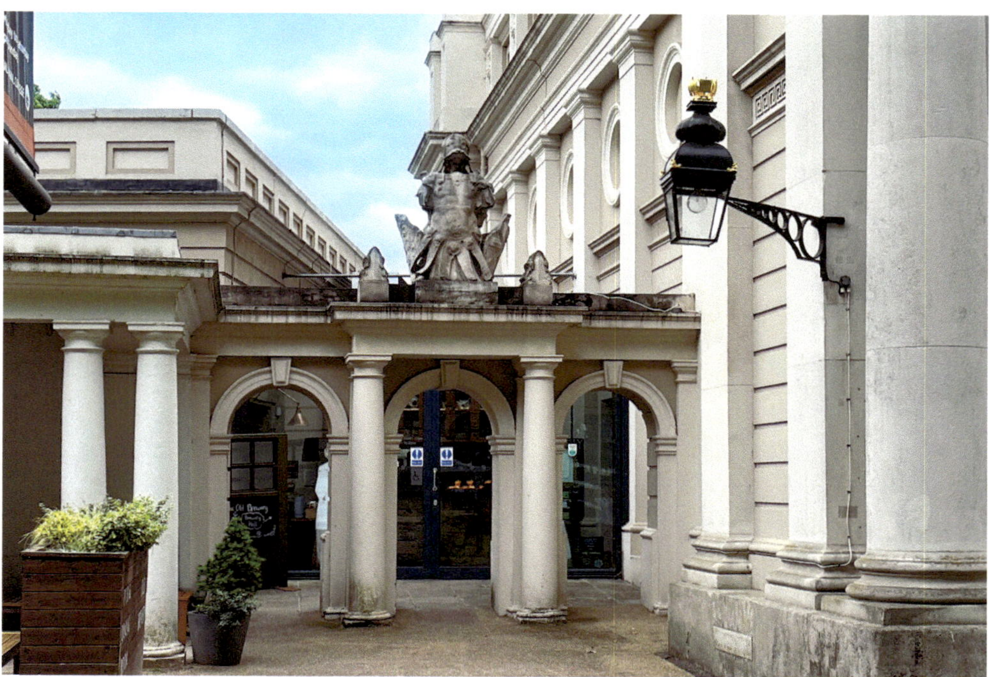

The Old Brewery on the site of Greenwich Hospital brewhouse.

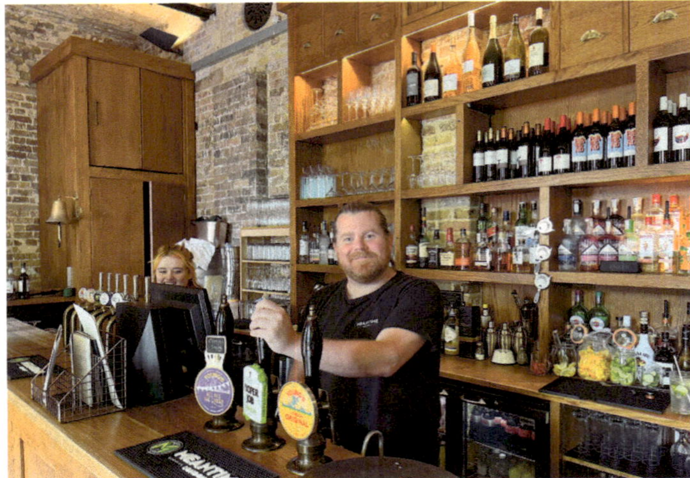

The Old Brewery's assistant manager Adam Gibson.

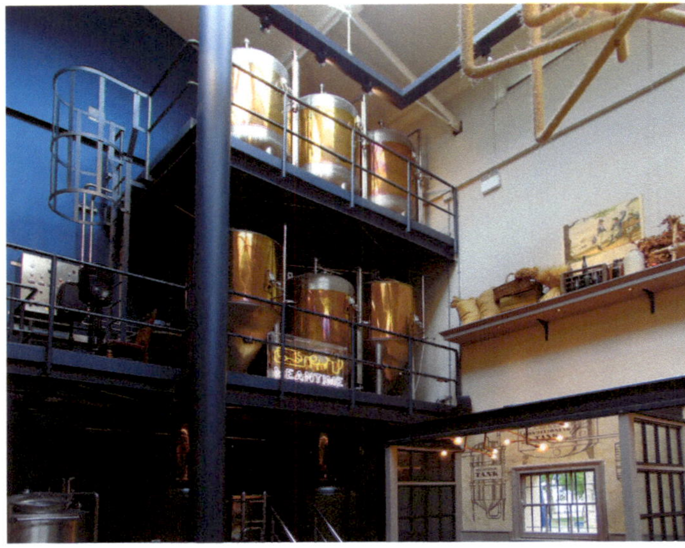

Copper barrels left in situ when brewing ceased at the Old Brewery.

After Meantime expanded their brewing industry during the early 2000s, they moved into the Pepys Building and opened the bar, restaurant, and brewery in 2010. The first beers brewed included a restorative Hospital Porter, using a recipe from the 1750s, and a Belgian Abbey Ale. Although the bars are not large, in good weather there is ample room outside in the beer yard, which seats well over 150 patrons. Overlooking the grounds of the Old Royal Naval College, from the yard you can see riverboats and coastal ships moving back and forth along the Thames, and on occasion even a naval warship sailing by.

Meantime ceased brewing on the premises before Youngs acquired the Old Brewery in 2016, spending £1 million on refurbishment. The large copper-clad brewing barrels were retained in place, now on display as a curious interior design feature.

THE TRAFALGAR TAVERN, Park Row

Erected on the site of the Old George, a small riverside pub used mostly by fishermen, the Trafalgar Tavern became famous for its ministerial whitebait dinners, served to Liberal Members of Parliament, and was often frequented by author and social critic Charles Dickens, and associates of the literary, art and theatrical fraternity.

The first licensee, Charles Hart, opened the tavern's doors to nobility, gentry, and the general public in 1837, the three-storey elegantly styled Regency building, with its grandeur furbished interior, comprised of drinking areas and dining rooms named after great naval victories or famous naval officers. The Trafalgar Tavern also had a coffee room, the drinking of coffee becoming a popular past-time during the nineteenth century, and private chambers for overnight accommodation, and adjacent to the main building the tavern had its own coach yard and stables.

Designed by architect Joseph Kay, clerk of works to Greenwich Hospital, and named to commemorate Nelson's famed victory at the Battle of Trafalgar, the tavern is featured as a setting for a wedding breakfast in Dickens's last novel, *Our Mutual Friend*. The Trafalgar Tavern became a popular destination for travellers arriving at Greenwich by boat, coach, and train to visit the riverside town's theatres, music halls, park, and celebrated historic landmarks. After the death of Hart, the tavern, under a succession of landlords, fell into less than favourable times, and was taken over by the Admiralty in 1915. Before the Second World War the tavern was briefly in use as an unemployment centre, and after the war it was a home for retired sailors, before coming into use as quarters for Royal Naval officers attending the nearby Royal Naval College.

The Trafalgar Tavern riverside.

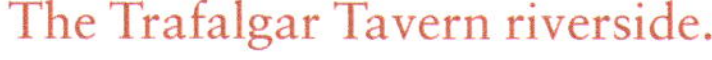

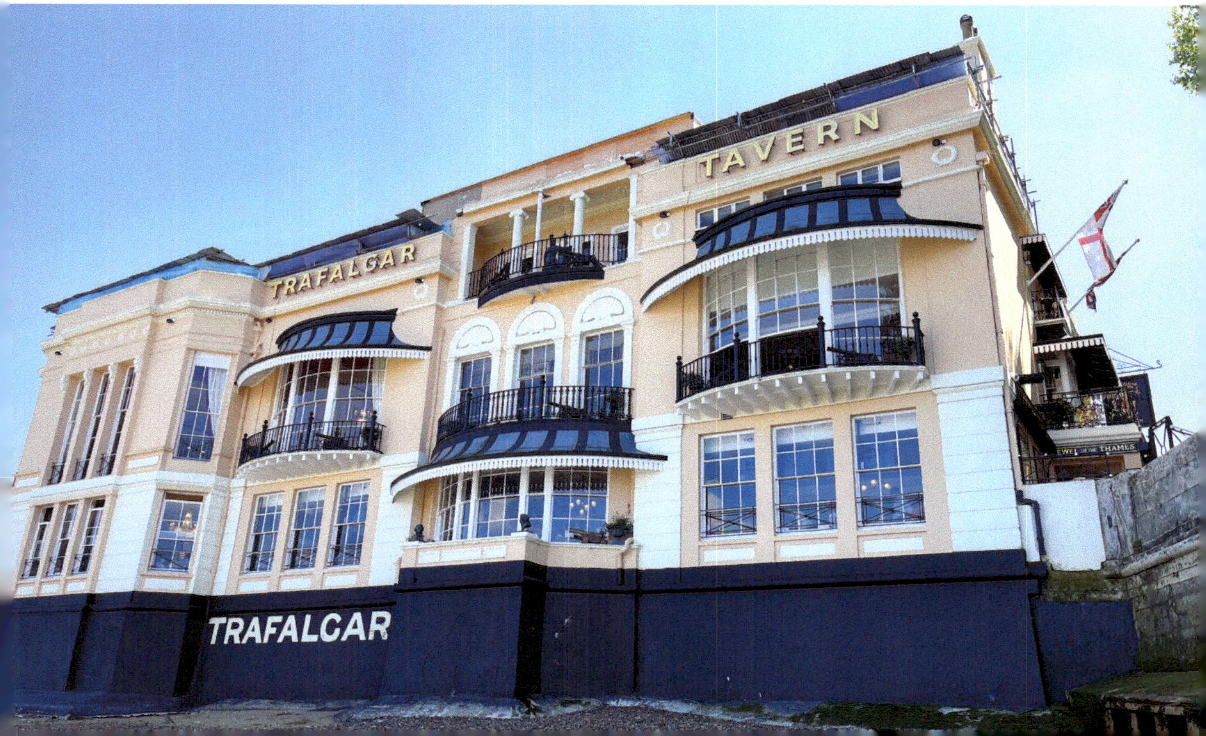

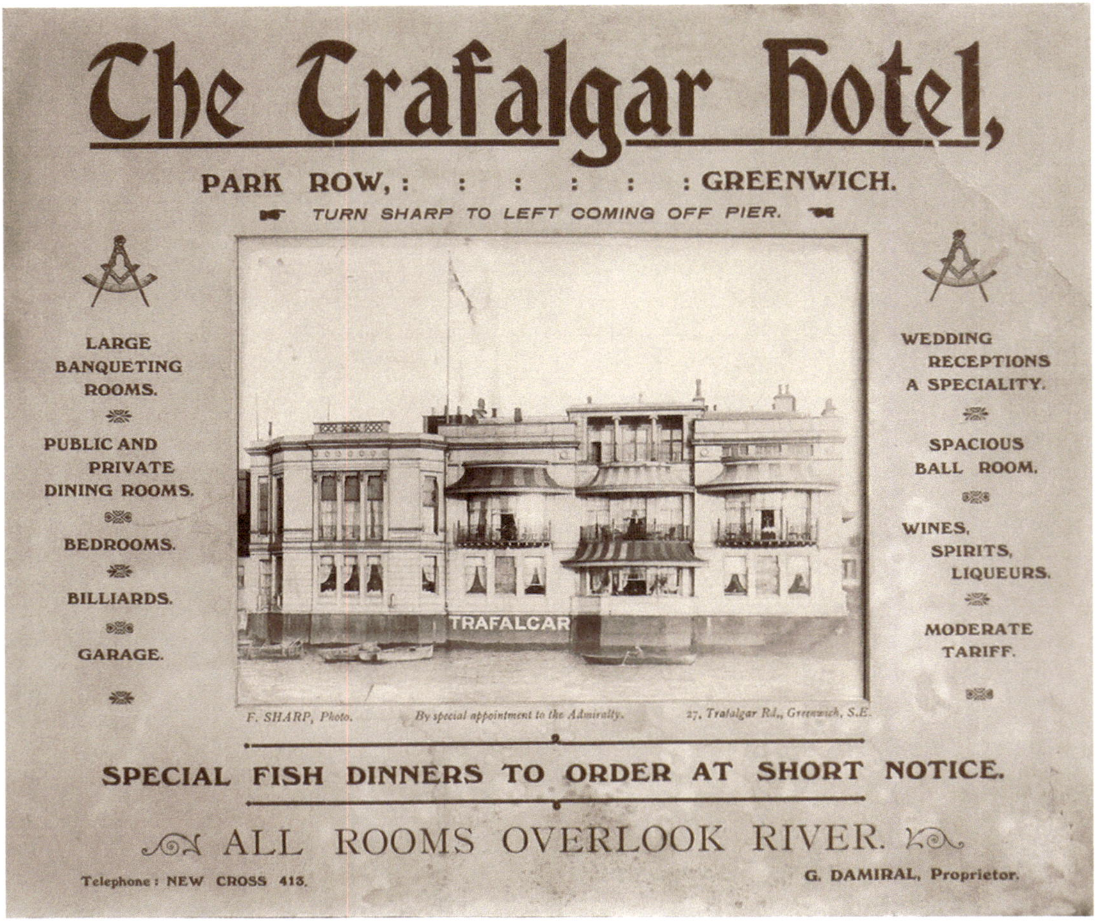

The Trafalgar Hotel,

PARK ROW, : : : : : GREENWICH.

TURN SHARP TO LEFT COMING OFF PIER.

LARGE BANQUETING ROOMS.

PUBLIC AND PRIVATE DINING ROOMS.

BEDROOMS.

BILLIARDS.

GARAGE.

F. SHARP, Photo.   By special appointment to the Admiralty.   27, Trafalgar Rd., Greenwich, S.E.

WEDDING RECEPTIONS A SPECIALITY.

SPACIOUS BALL ROOM.

WINES, SPIRITS, LIQUEURS.

MODERATE TARIFF.

SPECIAL FISH DINNERS TO ORDER AT SHORT NOTICE.

ALL ROOMS OVERLOOK RIVER.

Telephone: NEW CROSS 413.   G. DAMIRAL, Proprietor.

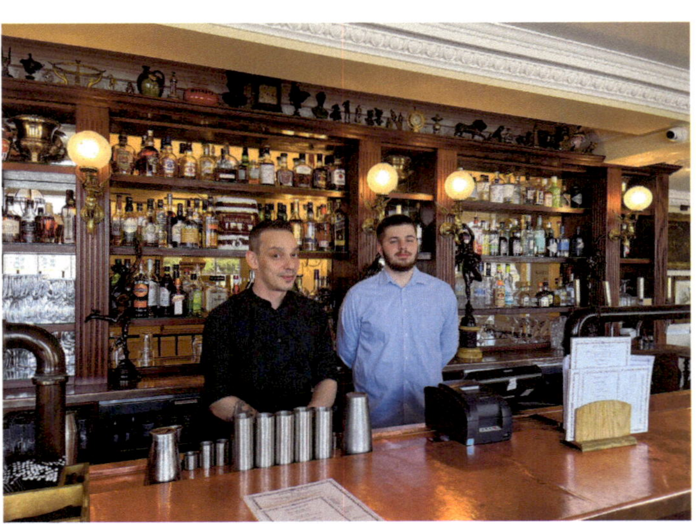

Above: Advertisement for the Trafalgar Tavern, early 1900s.

Left: General manager of the Trafalgar Tavern Vasil Vasilov and his supervisor Joe.

Restored in 1968 to its former glory of Victorian times, and refurbished several times since, the Trafalgar Tavern is the only remaining survivor of the grandeur riverside establishments of a bygone age, celebrating its past with a fascinating collection of period artifacts and artworks displayed in its spacious bars and dining areas, where whitebait is still served, although not exclusively to ministers of parliament.

THE YACHT, Crane Street

Situated to the centre of a narrow walkway, and overlooking the Thames, the Yacht, which dates to the late eighteenth century, originally named the Barley Mow and then the Waterman's Arms, is situated west of the Meridian Line in the historic Greenwich parish. Like much of the riverfront properties at this point, the Yacht has gone through a series of rebuilds and refurbishments over time and is one of very few existing riverside pubs to be found in Greenwich.

Around the mid-1960s, the pub's interior was remodelled to resemble a lounge bar aboard the cruise liner *Queen Mary*, and an extension was later added to enclose an open garden area to the rear between the pub and river.

Once frequented by riverside workers, lightermen and watermen, as the working environment changed along the river after the Second World War, and through the mid to late 1900s, apartments gradually replaced riverside work spaces. The Yacht attracted new custom, residents moving into the area, along with tourist who now visit Greenwich throughout the year.

The Yacht Tavern overlooking the Thames.

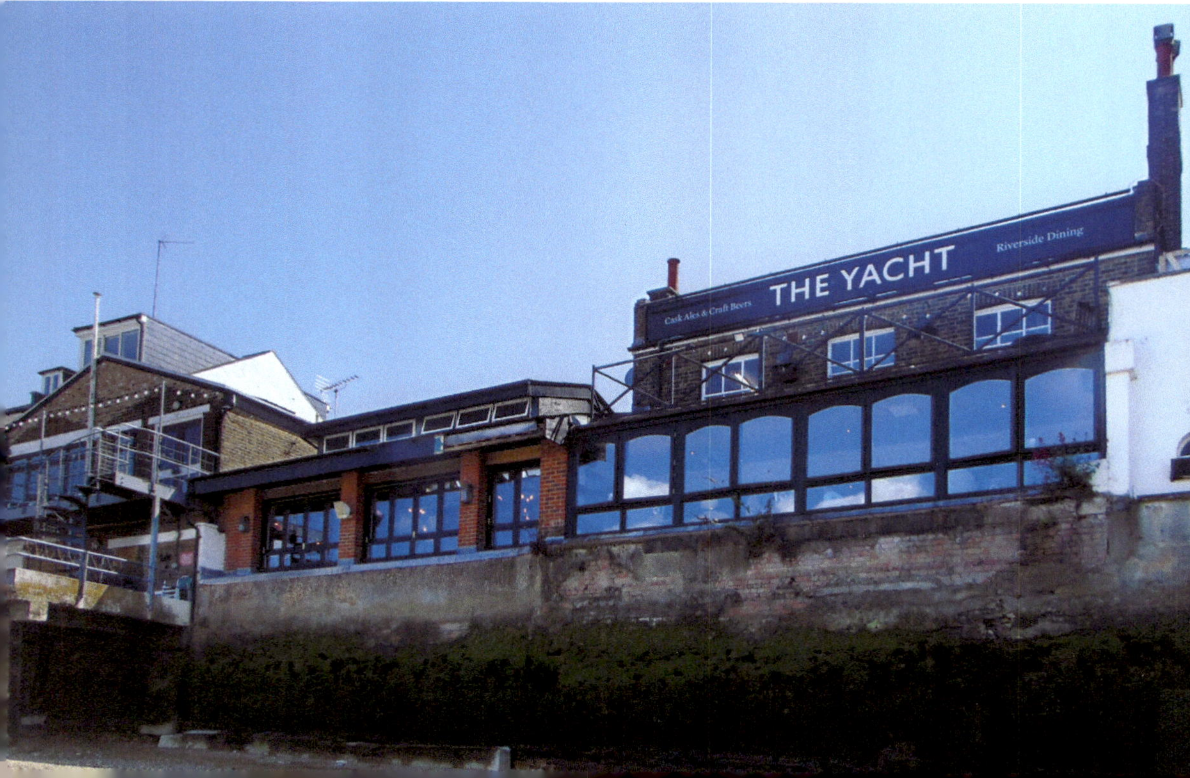

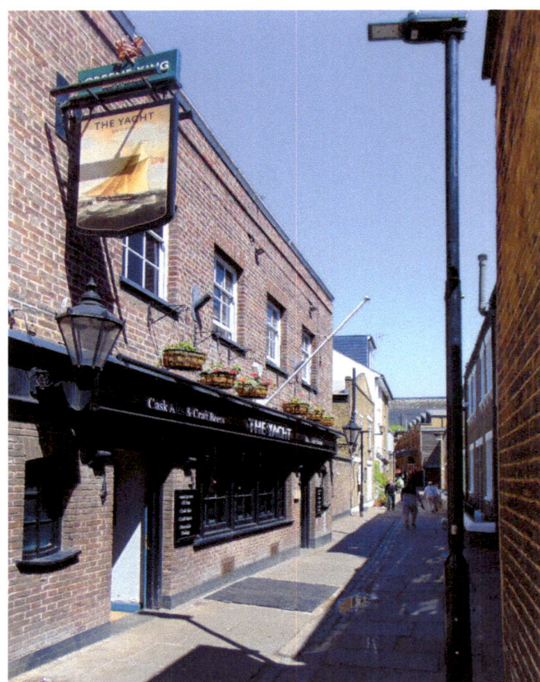

The Yacht Tavern entrance on Crane Street.

The oldest rowing club on the Tideway, Curlew, formerly known as Curley, founded in 1866, had been based at various boathouses in Greenwich for over 150 years, and their current headquarters is located at the Trafalgar Rowing Centre on Crane Street, on the same side as the Yacht, where crews would go for a beer after a rowing session out on the Thames. The rowing club also once stored boats on Corbett's pontoon, adjacent to the rear of the Yacht, where you could watch the boat crews setting off on the river.

Now under the ownership of Greene King, the Yacht has become as well known for serving a variety of meals as it has for offering a wide selection of beers and cocktails where you can sit overlooking the Thames, while drinking and eating, and occasionally still see boat crews rowing past.

Although there is certainly a different kind of atmosphere when visiting the Yacht today, compared to when the pub was frequented by river workers, you may still encounter a few old pensioners from Trinity Hospital Almshouses, who when out for an afternoon pint, the Yacht being their closest pub, can tell a few stories about the working riverside from days gone by.

THE CUTTY SARK, Ballast Quay

The origins of the Cutty Sark pub date back to the early eighteenth century, when land adjacent to the river had been known as Dog Kennel Meadow, before the building of houses and layout of streets. Various commercial and public properties were erected along the riverfront, including a pub, named the Green Man, up until the turn of the century.

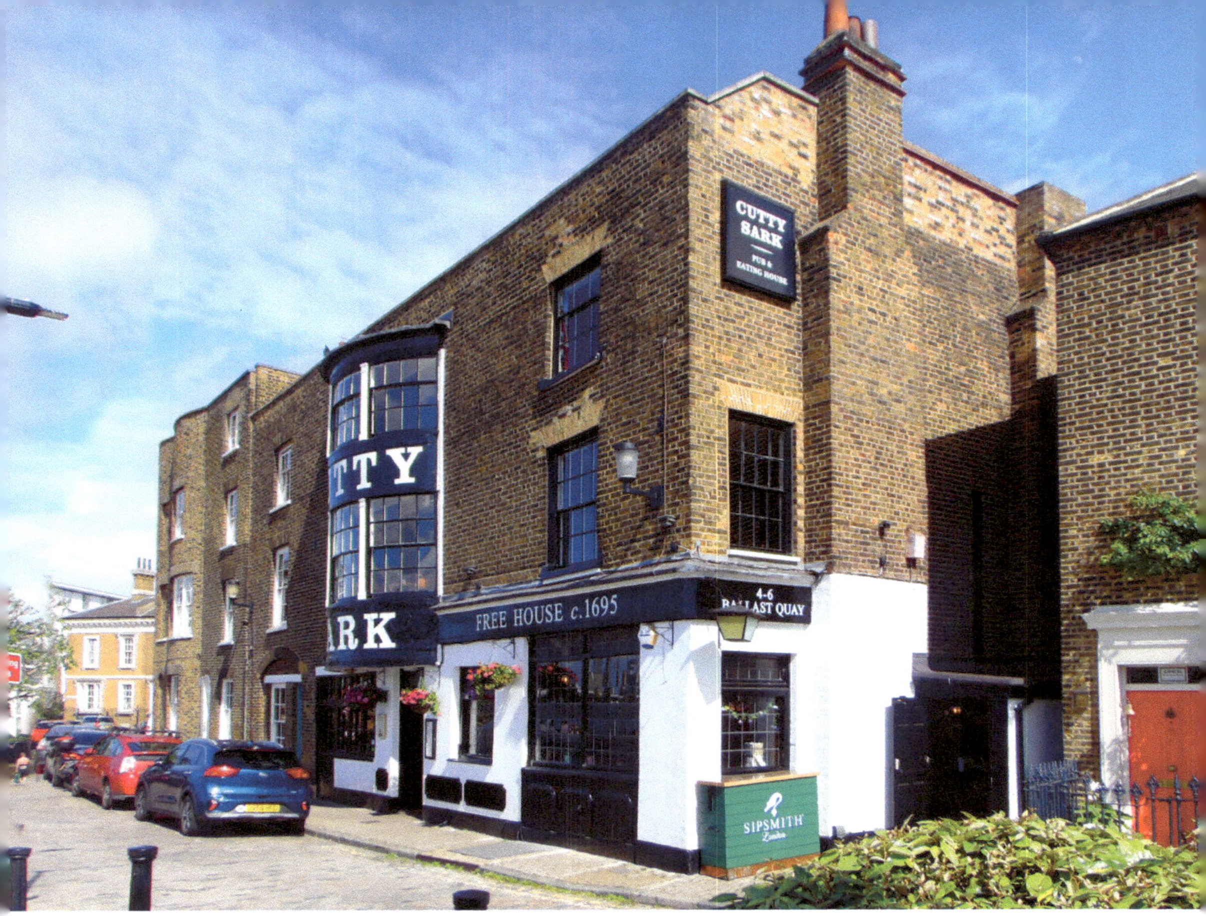

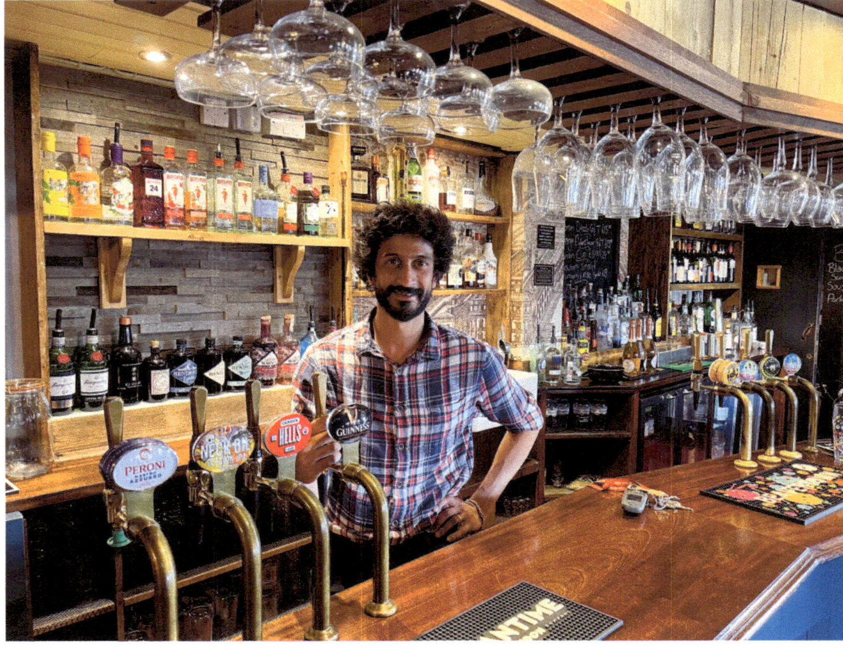

Above: The Cutty Sark riverside.

Right: General manager of the Cutty Sark Alex Sen.

A majority of land at this time was owned by Morden College, a charitable organisation established by philanthropist Sir John Morden in 1695 to provide care for merchants who had fallen on hard times, the charity investing in land purchases to raise income through rents and leases.

Demolished around the late 1700s, along with the adjoining buildings, the pub was rebuilt and renamed the Union Tavern, believed to commemorate the Union of England and Ireland in 1801. Positioned on a stretch of the Thames that was constantly busy with river traffic over the following two centuries, vessels loading and unloading cargo and taking on ballast dug from Blackheath, from which Ballast Quay takes its name, the pub became a popular drinking hole for river workers and crews of boats, coasters and ships mooring on the Thames.

After the arrival of the clipper ship *Cutty Sark* to Greenwich in 1951, the Union changed its name to the Cutty Sark, no doubt to cash in on the historic sailing ship's popularity, and the expected increase of visitors coming to Greenwich. Ten years on the pub found fame in a Hollywood murder mystery film, *The List of Adrian Messenger*, directed by John Huston and featuring stars of the silver screen, Tony Curtis, Burt Lancaster, Robert Mitchum and Frank Sinatra, all appearing in disguise, alongside Kirk Douglass and George C. Scott. The exterior and interior of the Cutty Sark featured in various scenes, and some of my friends were drafted in as film extras, portraying a group of young local Greenwich scallywags running down the cobbled street.

Before fully refurbished in the 1980s, the Cutty Sark, now one in a chain of Young's pubs, was where you could encounter a gathering of Greenwich's more colourful characters, including a local resident who enjoyed a drink in one of its two bars, accompanied by a parrot perched on her shoulder.

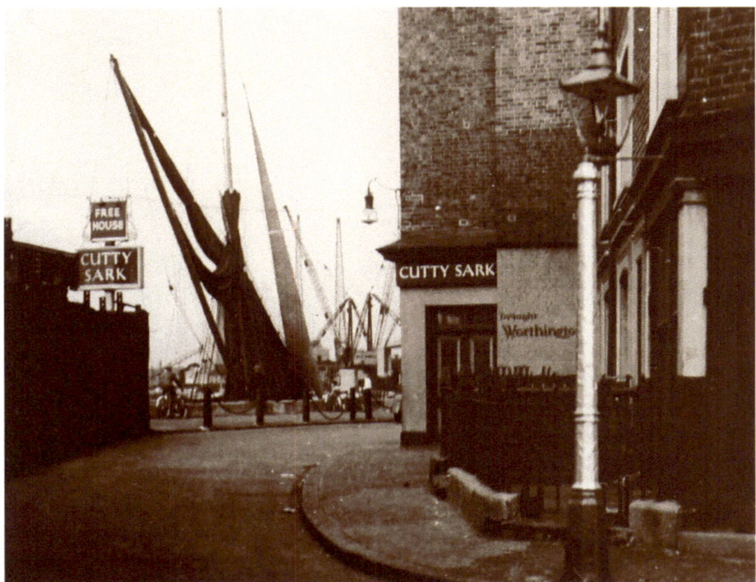

The Cutty Sark,
mid-1900s.

As the riverside industries eventually disappeared, replaced by new build riverside residential properties, Cutty Sark's clientele, made up of tourists, day trippers and new residents, have replaced the riverside labour force of stevedores, lightermen, watermen and merchant seamen who could once be found enjoying a few pints at the end of their hard day's work on the river.

ENDERBY HOUSE, Enderby Wharf

Another in the Young's pub chain, Grade II Enderby House was formerly an early nineteenth-century residential property owned by the Enderbys, a family of merchants and whalers, built at a site acquired by Samuel Enderby II for the manufacture of rope and canvas to supply the Enderbys' fleet of whaling ships.

The Enderby's became London's largest whaling company funding several pioneering expeditions into the Southern Ocean, leading to the discovery of the Bellany Islands and the founding of the Enderby Settlement at Port Ross, to the north-east of the Auckland Islands. Major-General Charles Gordon, born at Woolwich in 1833, married into the Enderby family when taking Elizabeth Enderby as his bride at a wedding ceremony which took place at Greenwich in 1873. After serving in various military campaigns in Eastern Europe, China and the Sudan, Gordon spent his last night in Britain at Enderby House, before dispatched to defend Khartoum, where he lost his life but became a national hero.

After many successful years trading, the money invested in the unproductive Enderby Settlement brought about the Enderby company's financial ruin and eventual liquidation.

Enderby House riverside.

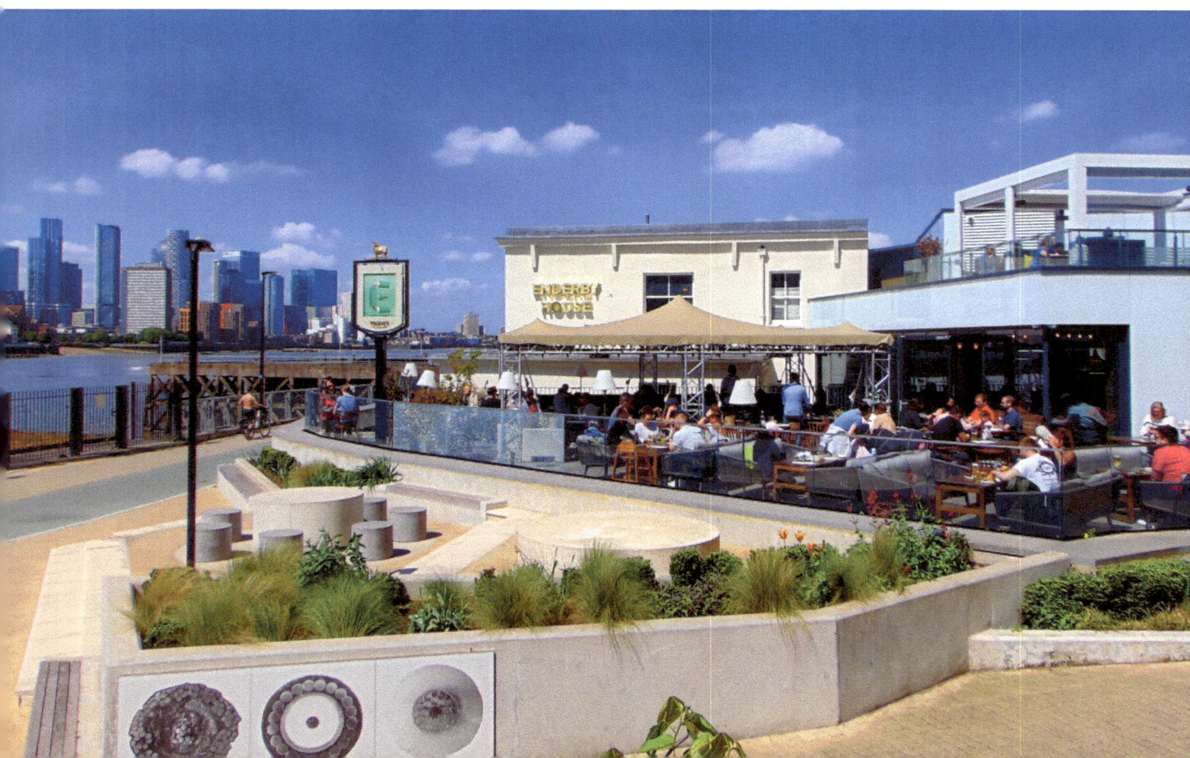

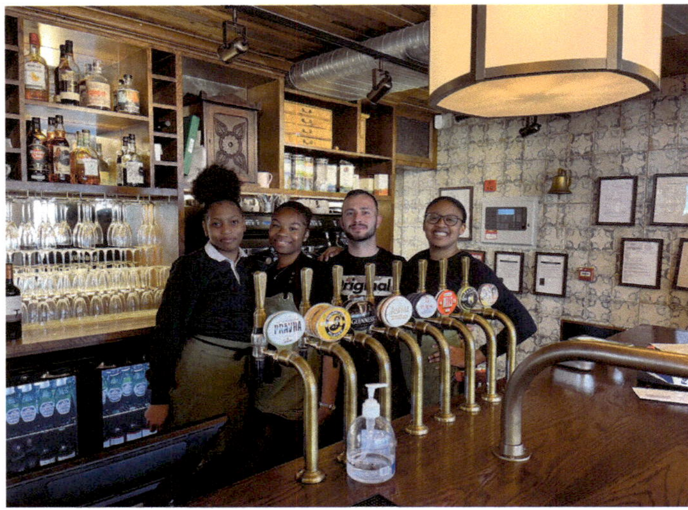

Enderby House staff members Amari, Danielle, Veselin and Jennifer.

The site, along with Enderby House, was sold on to Glass, Elliott & Co. for the production of submarine telegraph communication cables, including the first subsea cable successfully laid across the Atlantic from Britain to America.

Glass, Elliott & Co. merged with the Telegraph Construction and Maintenance Company, and when part of the site at Enderby's Wharf was sold for redevelopment, Enderby House, then used as offices, fell into a state of decay.

Local groups campaigned to save the celebrated property, which has important links to the historic industries and technological innovations associated with Greenwich Marsh, and the house was acquired by Young's in 2019, for restoration and refurbishment as a pub and restaurant.

The original house, consisting of two buildings, required extensive renovation and alterations, and a new modern extension was added to expand the floor space, the interior designed and furnished to reflect the building's historic significance to subsea telegraphy and heritage of the Enderby family.

With plans to erect more new residential properties in the surrounding area of Greenwich Marsh, once a centre of industry and mercantile commerce, Enderby House will have no shortage of clientele with hundreds of new residents moving to Greenwich Peninsula, many having a pint while using their mobile phone or tablet, unaware they are at the centre of where global network communications first began.

MORDEN WHARF TAPROOM, Morden Wharf

Occupying a mid-twentieth-century red-brick-built riverside warehouse, the modern day taproom brewery and outdoor music venue, under the management of Brew By Numbers, opened over the 2022 May Bank Holiday weekend.

On the edge of the Thames bank in the historical industrial area of Greenwich, the spacious building, with an open air terrace and views of Canary Wharf and passing river traffic, can accommodate around 500 people inside and outside. The furnishings, seating

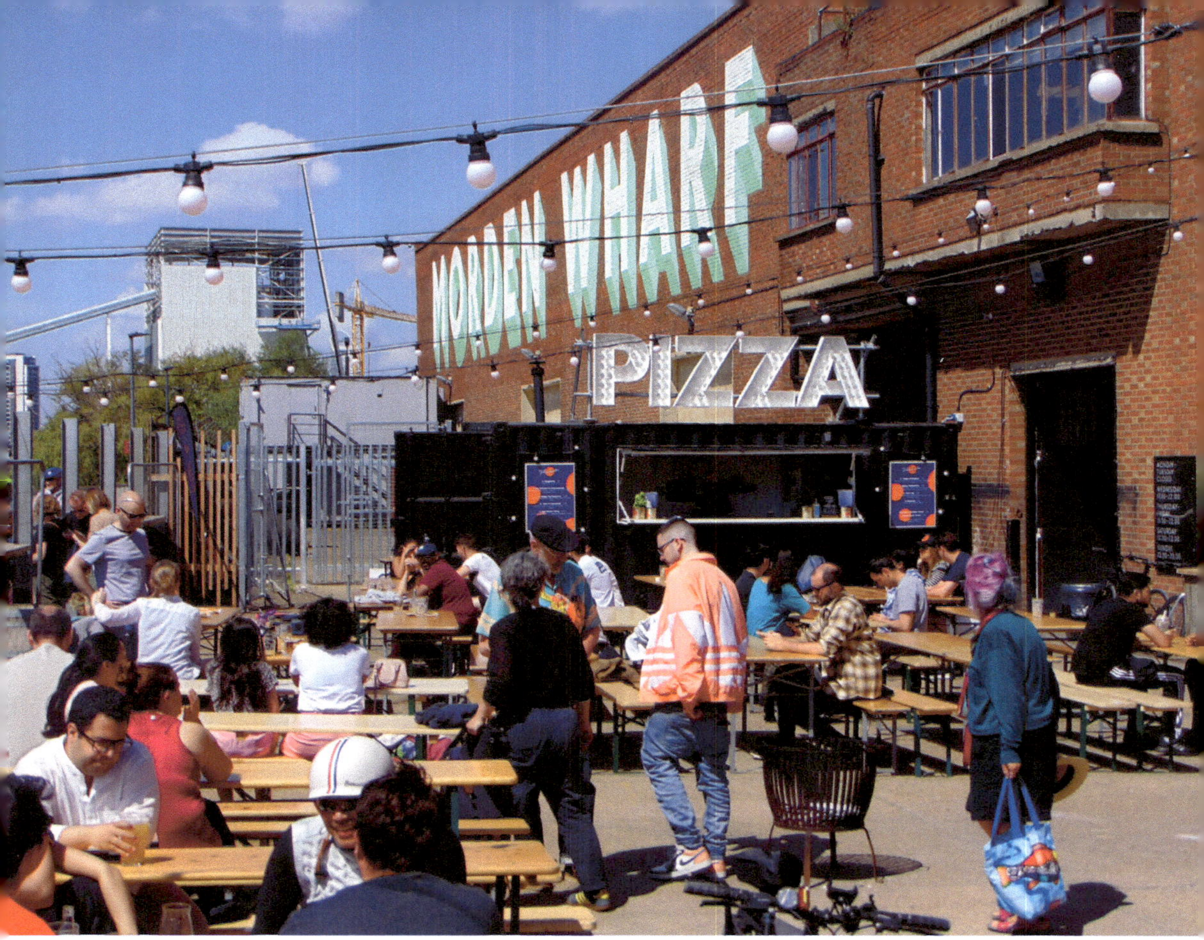

Above: Morden
Wharf Taproom
terrace riverside.

Right: The manager
of Morden
Wharf Taproom
Jason Rogers.

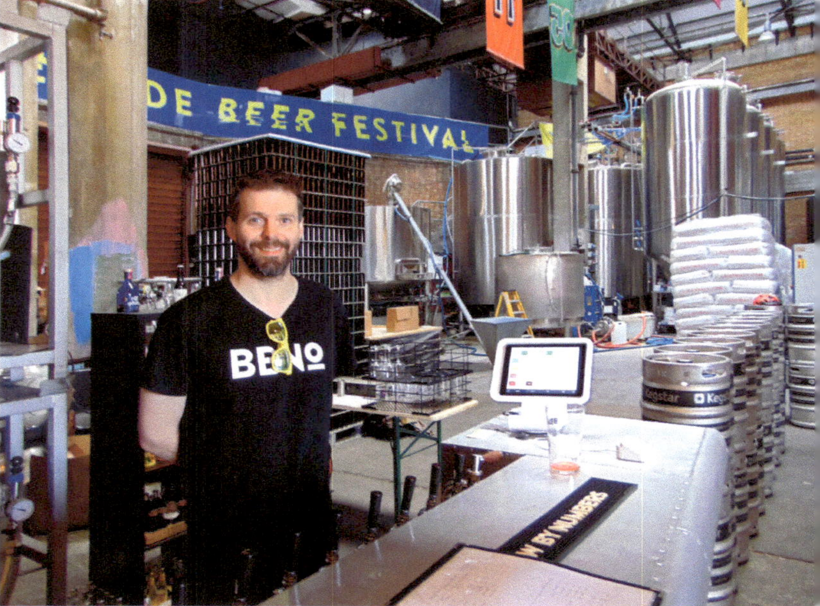

and tables are made from reclaimed timber. Serving a variety of beers brewed on the premises, the taproom also offers a range of cocktails, and wood-fired pizza street food is available from the terrace mega-cool van. Morden Wharf Taproom hosts international DJs playing a mix of sounds to drink and dine by, or dance to, with a large outdoor HD screen for live sporting events and celebratory broadcasts, and a space for live music sessions.

Morden Wharf is now part of a large mixed-use development project on an industrial site that was once home to shipbuilders and boatbuilders, soap makers and rope makers, and after the Second World War, a cement works, scrap metal merchants, and fertilizer and animal food refinery. Morden Wharf Taproom is the first stage of a new leisure quarter, comprising of a market square, cafés, and retail outlets.

THE PILOT, Ceylon Place

Before various commercial businesses evolved upon Greenwich Marsh, this large expanse of land to the north of Greenwich was used mainly for livestock grazing. Enclosed by an upward loop in the Thames, accessed by a single trackway, Marsh Lane, leading northwards from the old Woolwich Road, a majority of the land was owned by Morden College and Trinity Hospital charities.

In the early 1800s, George Russell acquired an area of marsh land to created New East Greenwich, consisting of a large corn tidal mill, and a row of millworkers terraced houses, Ceylon Place, with a public house, the Pilot, built at the end.

It is believed the pub took its name from the words of a song sung out at the inauguration of the Pitt Club, 'here's to the Pilot that Weathered the storm', a tribute to

The Pilot on Greenwich Marsh.

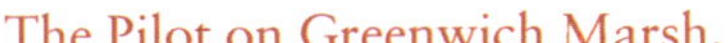

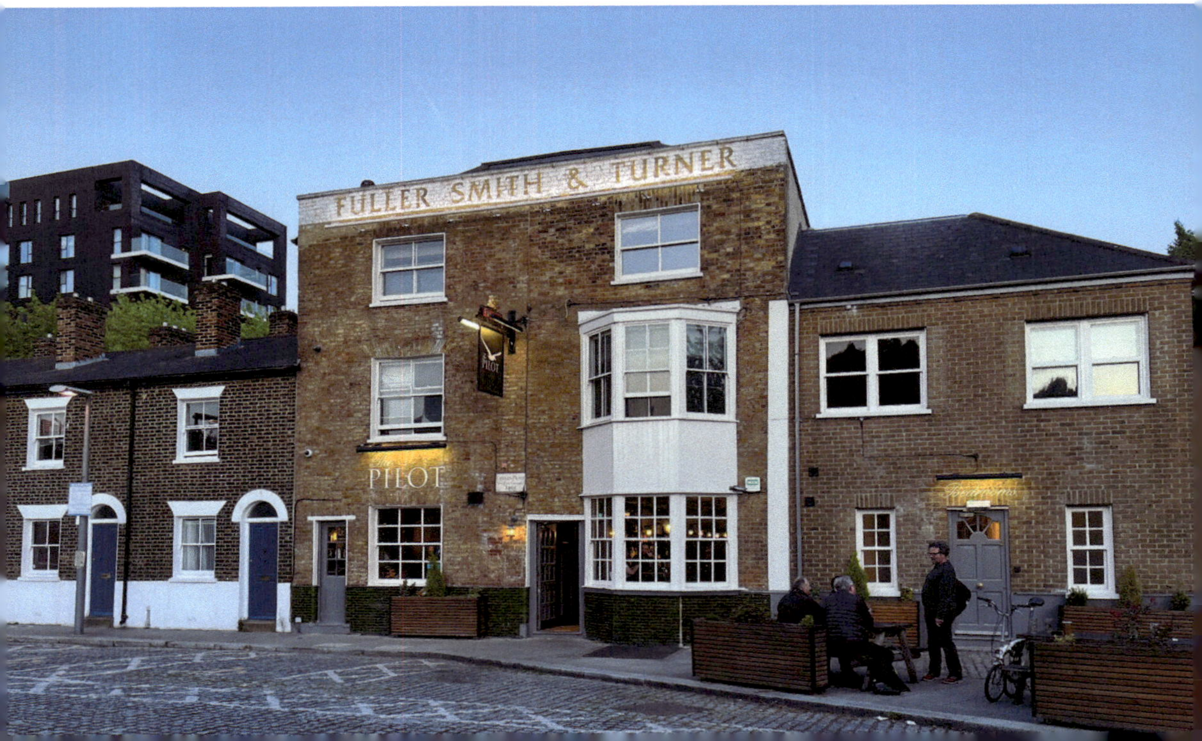

former Prime Minister William Pitt the Younger, who, along with his elder brother and several politicians, held land leases on the marsh.

The Pilot, one of several pubs built on Greenwich Marsh, was not only frequented by the millworkers but also by labourers employed in the many other local industries which evolved upon the marsh and along the river over the following two centuries. Before many of the riverside industries closed down, coastal vessels sailing from the north of Britain loaded with coal, along with freighters arriving with various cargo from foreign shores, would moor at Blackwall Reach, their crews mingling with the riverside workers at the Pilot, exchanging tobacco, cigarettes, various bottles of spirits, and even petrol between them, without the need to pay duty fees.

The Pilot was the first pub where I worked as a barman, for Irish landlord Tony, who gave me the job as a favour to my father, as both were friends, and during my time behind the bar I was witness to many of these transactions taking place, turning a blind eye for a bottle of Double Diamond.

During the regeneration of Greenwich Marsh, when the old industries were replaced by new urban village developments, rebranded Greenwich Peninsula, the Pilot, the last surviving original pub on the marsh, after being taken over by Fullers, was refurbished and enlarged to accommodate the expected increase of custom coming from residents moving to the Peninsula, and arrival of tourists and visitors attending concerts and sports events at the O2 Arena, Design District art and fashion shows, and shopping at the Icon Outlet.

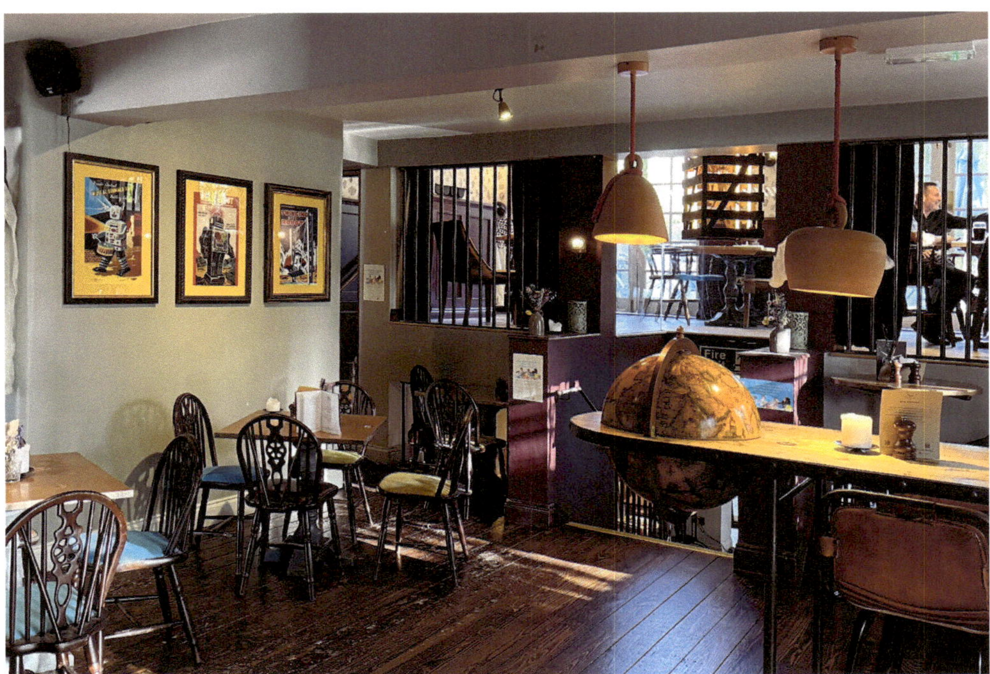

Main bar of the Pilot.

3

West Greenwich

Up until the mid-1600s, much of West Greenwich was made up of open land and fields, with a majority of buildings grouped around St Alphege's Church, Billingsgate Dock, along the Dover Road, and the most populated area, the medieval quarter adjacent to Greenwich Palace.

As Greenwich evolved over the following 200 years, buildings were erected each side of roads leading westwards from the town centre, which included several taverns and inns along the routes, and the ramshackle group of medieval structures were cleared to make way for elegantly built properties, four public houses and a market at the centre.

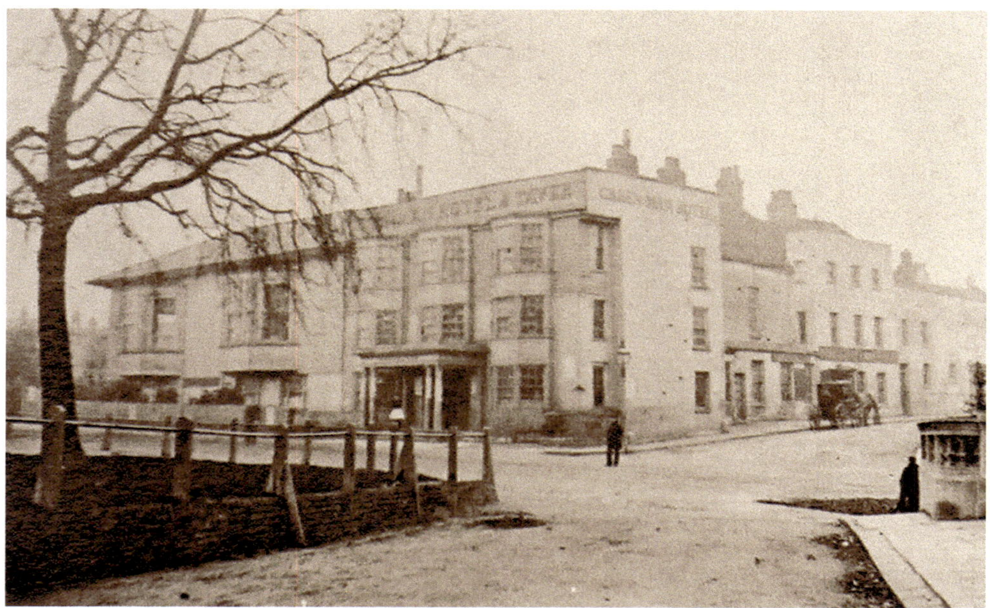

The Green Man, early 1900s, demolished to build flats in 1970.

Leading up a steep escarpment towards Blackheath, large palatial houses were built for sea captains, merchants, bankers, wealthy industrialists, artists, and musicians, and although there were very few new public houses erected amongst the elite of society, there already existed several coaching inns. These included the seventeenth-century Green Man, at the top of Blackheath Hill, once headquarters of Blackheath Golf Club and later a music venue where many of the top groups of the 1970s and 1980s played; the Horse & Groom, further down on Blackheath Hill, demolished in 2004 after the cellar collapsed into old chalk mining caverns; and towards the town centre to the bottom of Crooms Hill, the Spread Eagle, converted into a restaurant, and which has since closed.

There were also several other public houses situated along Blackheath Hill and Blackheath Road, on the very edge of the parish, including the Duchess of Kent, Prince of Wales, Sun, Yorkshire Grey, Royal Albert, and White Swan, pubs now either demolished, awaiting demolition or repurposing.

THE GATE CLOCK, Creek Road

As with a majority of cities and towns throughout the country, you will undoubtably come across a property which had fallen out of use, a cinema, bank, warehouse or public building, as well as a vacant space in a new build, acquired by the pub

The Gate Clock open all hours – almost.

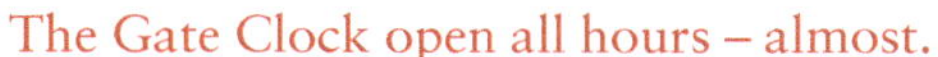

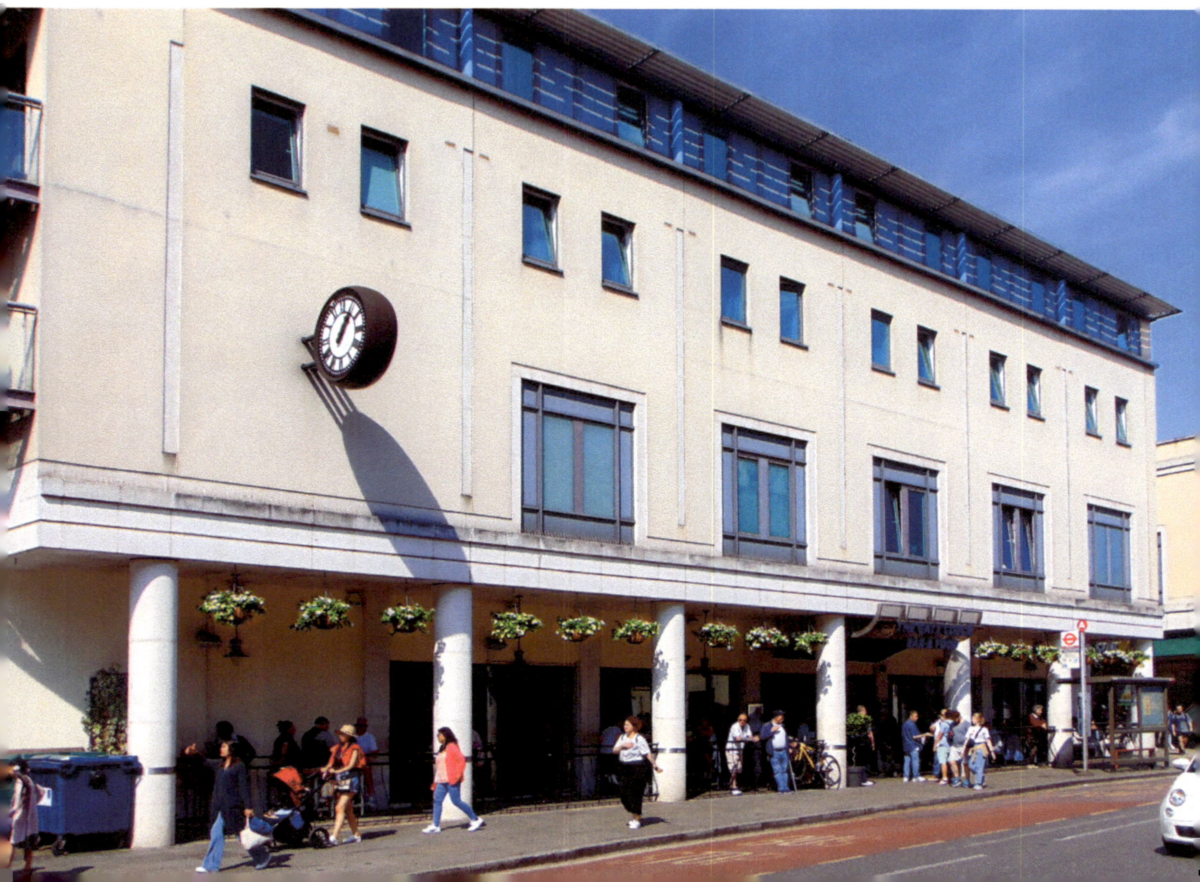

chain JD Wetherspoon, the structure converted and refurbished then reopened as a public house. The JD Wetherspoon at Greenwich, the Gate Clock, is located to the west of the town's centre on Creek Road, the original main highway leading toward London.

JD Wetherspoon, founded in 1979, which offers customers reduced prices on cask, draft, and bottled beers, along with wines and spirits, and a selection of inexpensive meals, makes use of a building's previous function, or in the case of a newly built property, a local landmark, in the pub's naming and interior design and decoration, which includes historical imagery, displays and information boards.

The Gate Clock was named after the twenty-four-hour Shepherd Gate Clock installed at the gates of the Royal Greenwich Observatory in 1852, the first electric clock to show Greenwich Mean Time. Opened in 2002, the Gate Clock occupies two floors of a contemporary building block, erected during a period of regeneration to the west of the historic Greenwich Market, replacing a row of dilapidated shops, the former buildings themselves erected on the remnants of medieval Greenwich. Attracting an assortment of international and occupational clientele, young people, students, tourists, commuters and a few local neighbourhood drinkers, the Gate Clock is close to Docklands Light Railway station and many of Greenwich's main historic attractions, the pub usually very busy throughout the summer, at weekends and festive occasions.

THE SPANISH GALLEON, Greenwich Church Street

When the medieval buildings at the centre of Greenwich were pulled down in the early 1830s, architect and Clerk of Works to Greenwich Hospital Joseph Kay incorporated a rebuilt pub, the Spanish Galleon, into his remodelled town centre, a large square of new Regency buildings surrounding a market square at the centre. It is believed a pub had existed on the corner of Clarence Street (College Approach) and Church Street since the seventeenth century.

The name, Spanish Galleon, most likely references Spanish ships depicted in paintings hanging on the walls of Greenwich Hospital, founded by Queen Mary II in 1692 as a permanent home for retired or disabled Royal Navy sailors.

Undoubtably many of these old pensioners would have taken a drink or two in the original pub while recalling seafaring tales of the times they boarded and captured Spanish galleons during times of war.

Although suffering some damage during the Blitz, the Spanish Galleon, which retains its exterior Regency architectural characteristics, was Grade II listed in 1973. While undergoing renovation in 1985, a well-preserved sailor's uniform was discovered in the cellar and placed on display in the bar. Managed by Britain's oldest brewer Shepherd Neame, established at Faversham in 1698, the Spanish Galleon has recently undergone further refurbishments, retaining its distinctive maritime theme and wealth of original interior architectural features. In between two large bars you will find Slap & Pickle, a modern brightly furbished booth area serving a variety of gourmet burgers and fries.

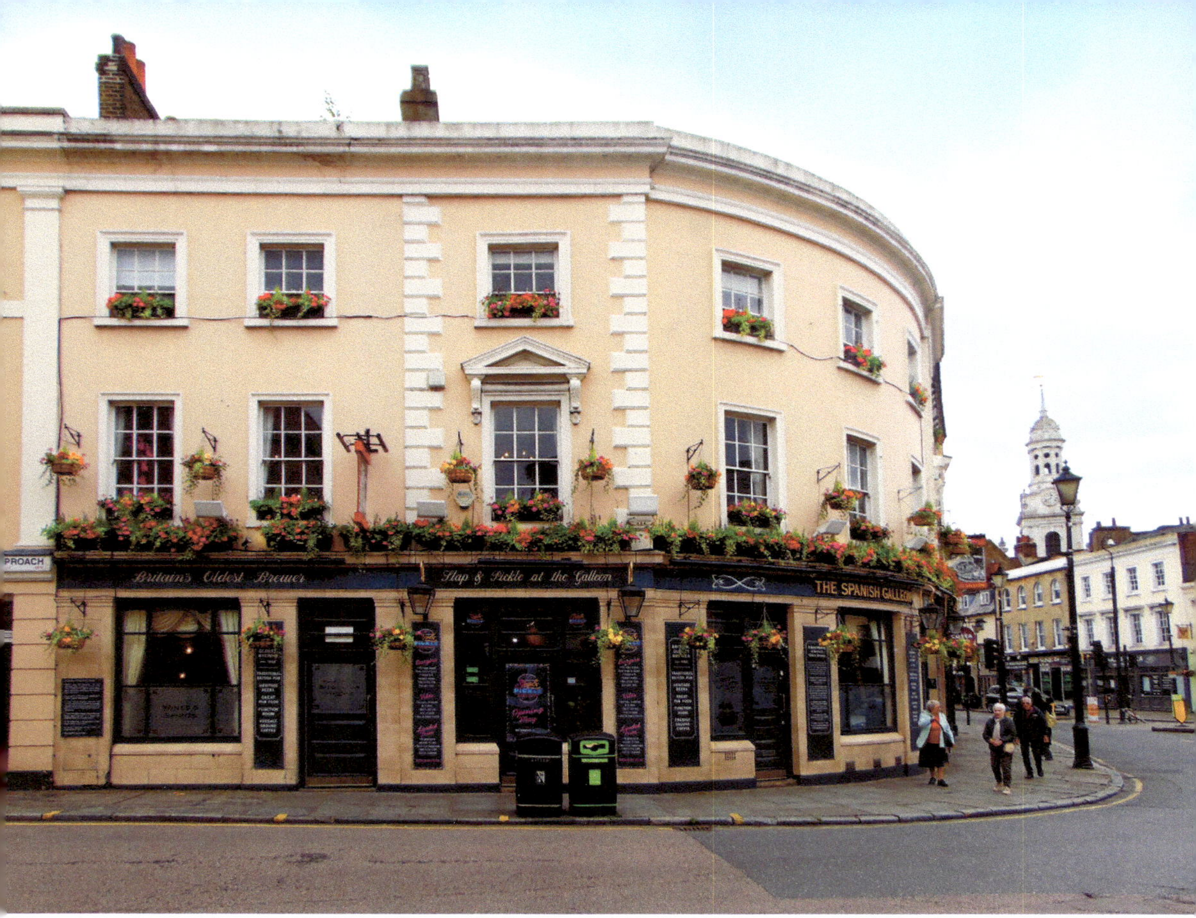

The Spanish Galleon after refurbishment in 2022.

THE ADMIRAL HARDY, College Approach

Named after Nelson's flag captain Admiral Hardy, commander of HMS *Victory* at Trafalgar, the pub was built on Clarence Street, now College Approach, during the redevelopment of the town centre by Greenwich Hospital estates and became a popular place to dine for visitors coming to Greenwich, where they could purchase a good dinner for about half a crown, equivalent to around £7 today, or an excellent tea for a shilling, equivalent to £3.[3]

To maximise income from the premises, a large room that had been erected over an arch leading into the market, which first received a performance licence in 1839, was converted into a music hall by licensee of the Admiral Hardy Henry Mitchell after obtaining permission from Greenwich Hospital in 1845. Known as the Admiral Hardy Music Hall, pub regulars, which included Greenwich Hospital pensioners, were encouraged by Mitchell to get up and take a turn singing a popular song of the day to entertain his paying patrons, who were also spending money on food and drink as well.

Refurbished in 1875, the music hall included a new stage, proscenium, balcony, and private boxes, and went by the title of the Clarence Music Hall and Bijou Theatre of

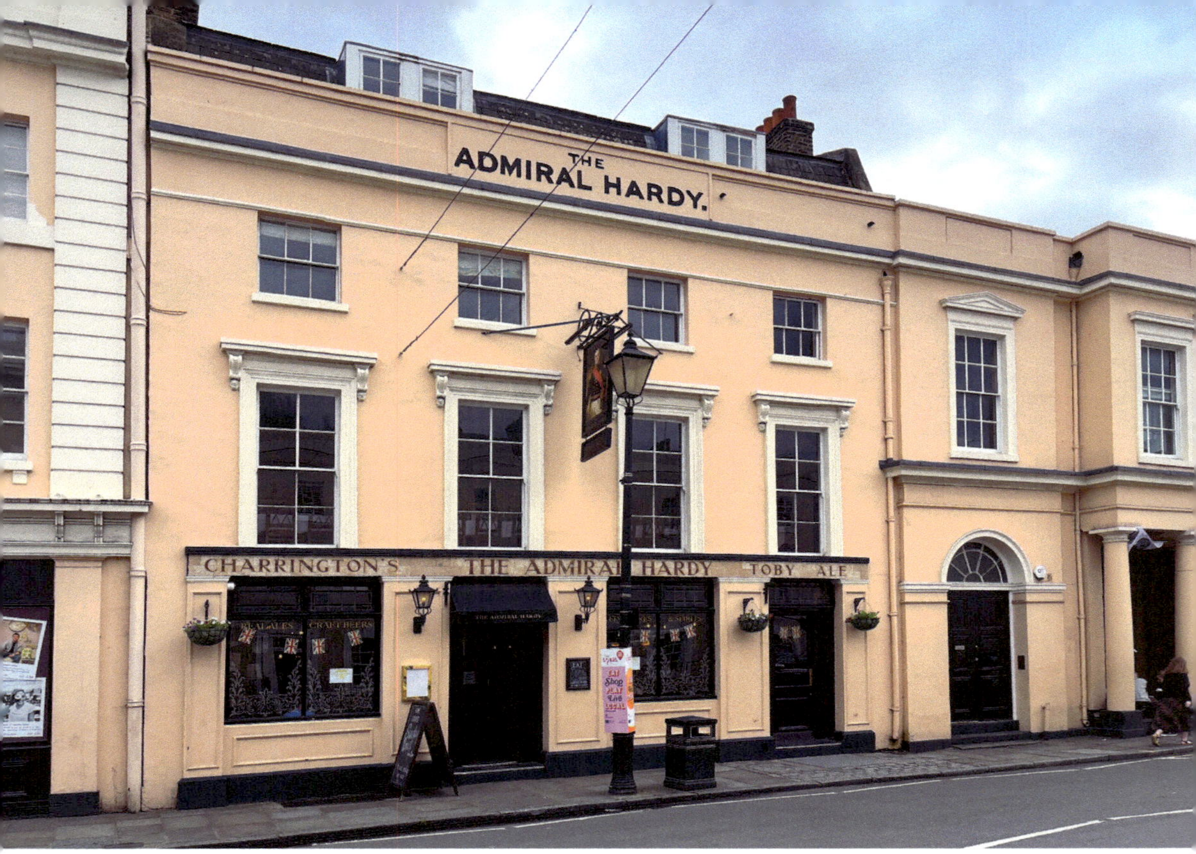

The Admiral Hardy, adjoining Greenwich Market.

Varieties. Performers included many of the most famous music hall artists of the age. Although the music hall closed in the late 1800s, the Admiral Hardy pub continued serving wines and beers to its customers, and like many other pubs during this period, rooms, or the whole pub, would be rented out as a place where local justice was conducted, which brought in extra income for the landlord.

On one such occasion, coroner Mr Carttar presided over an inquest into the death of William Glover, who died in the Seamen's Hospital from injuries received at Deptford Bridge on the night of Monday 30 May 1881, after the horse and cart he was driving overturned at the embankment where work on the tramway was being carried out. The jury returned a verdict of accidental death, but considered neglect was shown by the London Tramway Company in not providing additional means of safe conduct through their roadworks.

Frequented during the 1900s by naval officers training at the Royal Naval College, the name Admiral Hardy would have been well known through the service, as Hardy, famous for the part he played at the Battle of Trafalgar and long distinguished naval career, served as Governor of Greenwich Hospital from 1834 up until his death in 1839.

Recently undergoing a full refurbishment, the Admiral Hardy is now a pub and hotel, and the old music hall space is available to hire for functions.

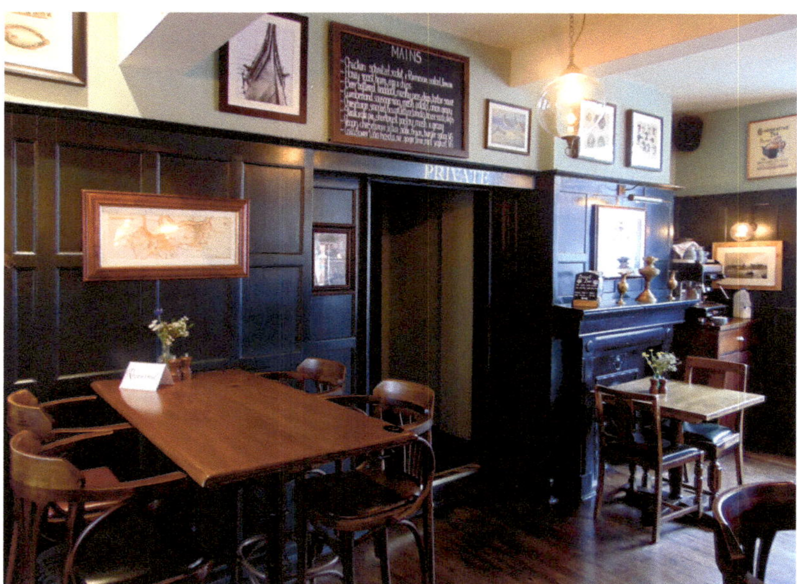

Nautical themed bar of the Admiral Hardy.

THE COACH & HORSES, Turnpin Lane

Located at the south-west corner of Greenwich Market, halfway along a narrow passageway, Turnpin Lane, once a medieval throughfare, you will find the Coach & Horses. Built in the late 1700s, believed to be named after the horse-drawn coaches arriving and departing from a nearby staging post, the pub has served market traders and their customers for over 300 years. In the late 1860s, the Coach & Horses, along with a consortium of other Kent pubs, began selling packs of tea, a direct response to grocers selling beer and wine, which had an impact on the pub trade.

Once an area where ne'er-do-wells and vagrants gathered, Victorian burglar and murderer Charlie Peace was believed to have had lodgings at Turnpin Lane while on the run from the law, most likely spending some of his ill-gotten gains in the Coach & Horses.

Throughout the twentieth century the pub has witnessed wholescale change around the market square. The vagabonds and market square vagrants have long gone, and from a time when market workers and traders were dealing with goods including livestock, poultry, meat, fish, eggs, butter, fruit, and vegetables, after a period of decline the market has transformed into a flourishing centre of arts, crafts, and antiques.

The Coach & Horses, with its outdoor covered seating area set out amongst the market stalls, has become an attractive and welcoming part of this lively and vibrant market quarter.

Serving a selection of beers and traditional pub grub, including Sunday roasts alongside gastro dishes, although no longer frequented by old time market regulars, the refurbished Coach an& Horses has become a popular and busy pub, not only during the summer months, but also throughout the year during market hours, as well as when the market holds community events and festive celebrations.

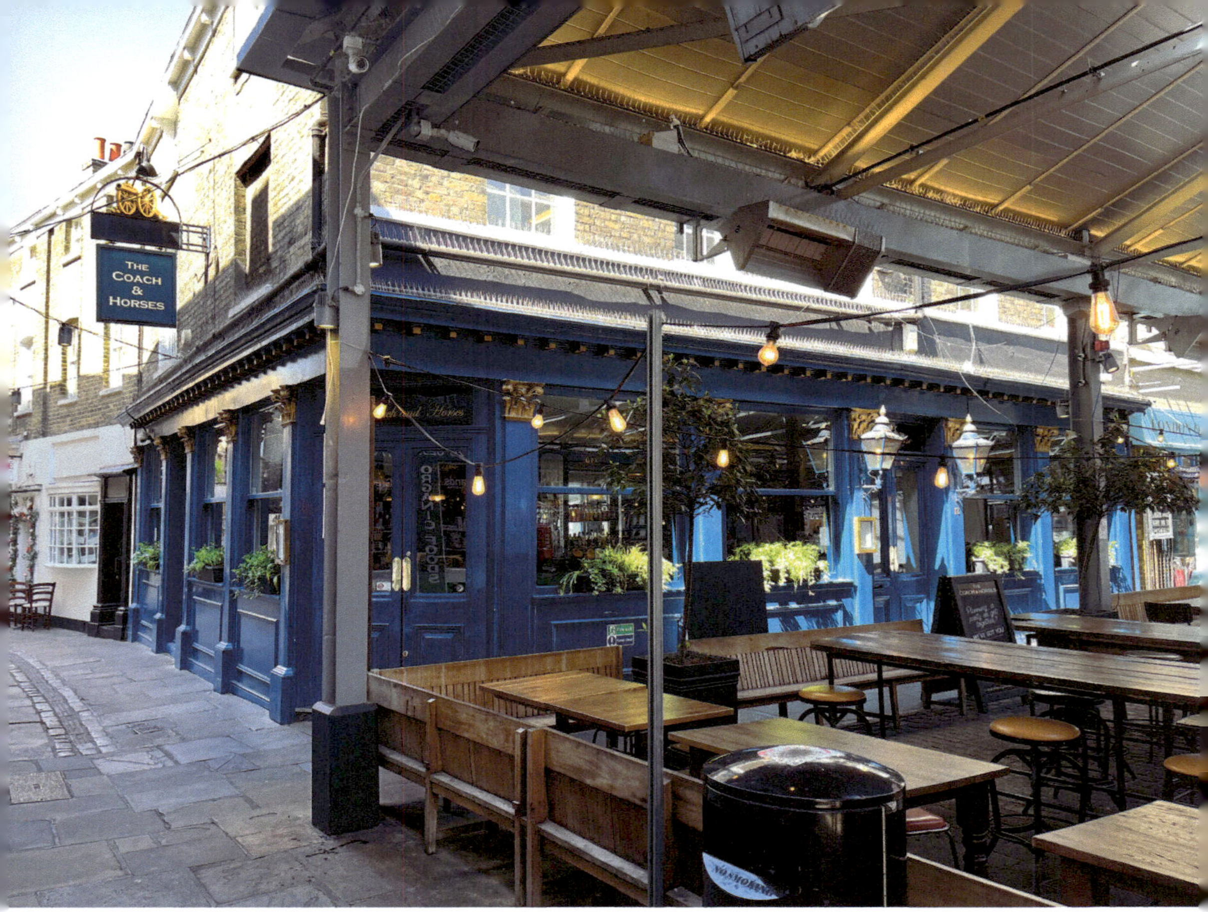

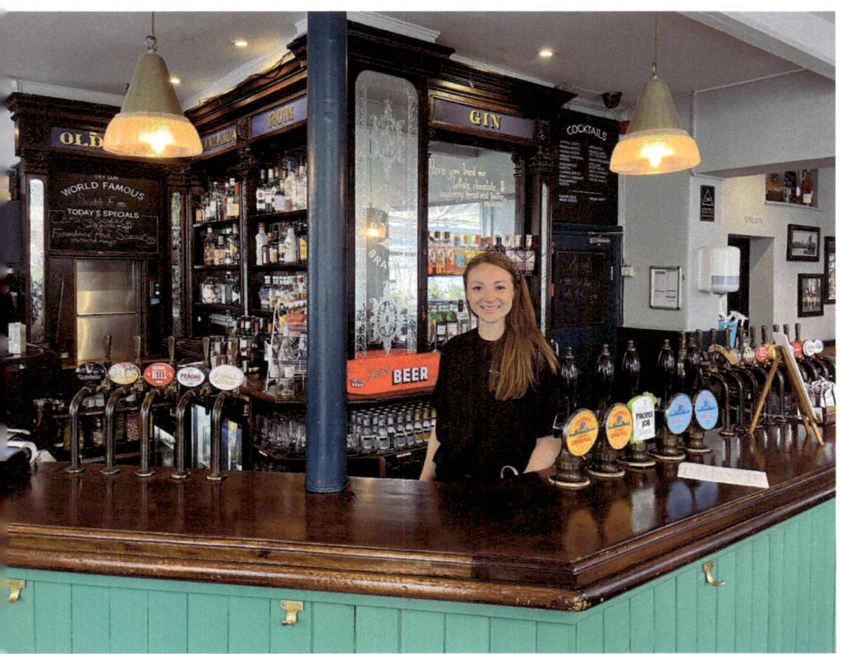

Above: The Coach & Horses located within Greenwich Market.

Left: The Coach & Horses' general manager Alana.

THE KINGS ARMS, King William Street

Known by some of the older local Greenwich drinkers as The Bunker, the Kings Arms dates back to the early 1800s, situated in a row of properties on the west side of the main route to and from Greenwich Park, formerly known as Rumley's Road. The pub has gone through various alterations and refurbishment since this time.

The thoroughfare was then renamed King Street, and during the 1930s, the name changed to King William Walk, a statue of King William IV resited from its location near London Bridge to a site close to the park's St Mary's Gate at the southern end of the road.

Although displaying the royal coat of arms on a sign board above the pub's main front entrance, it is not known if the Kings Arms has any associations to a specific king. The pub's nickname, however, has a more interesting history.

The name Bunker is believed to have been used from a time when labourers shovelling coal at nearby power stations would take some refreshment at the pub between shifts, leaving their shovels lined up outside the door. The name was then further cemented into the pubs history during the Second World War after its regulars would descend to the cellar, the bunker, during air raids to carry on drinking their beer.

A favourite drinking place for naval staff of the Royal Naval College, which included a young Prince Charles, a king in waiting at the time, the pub was also referred to as the Bunker by trainee naval officers, and by many local residents well into the 1980s.

The Kings Arms, favourite boozer of Prince Charles.

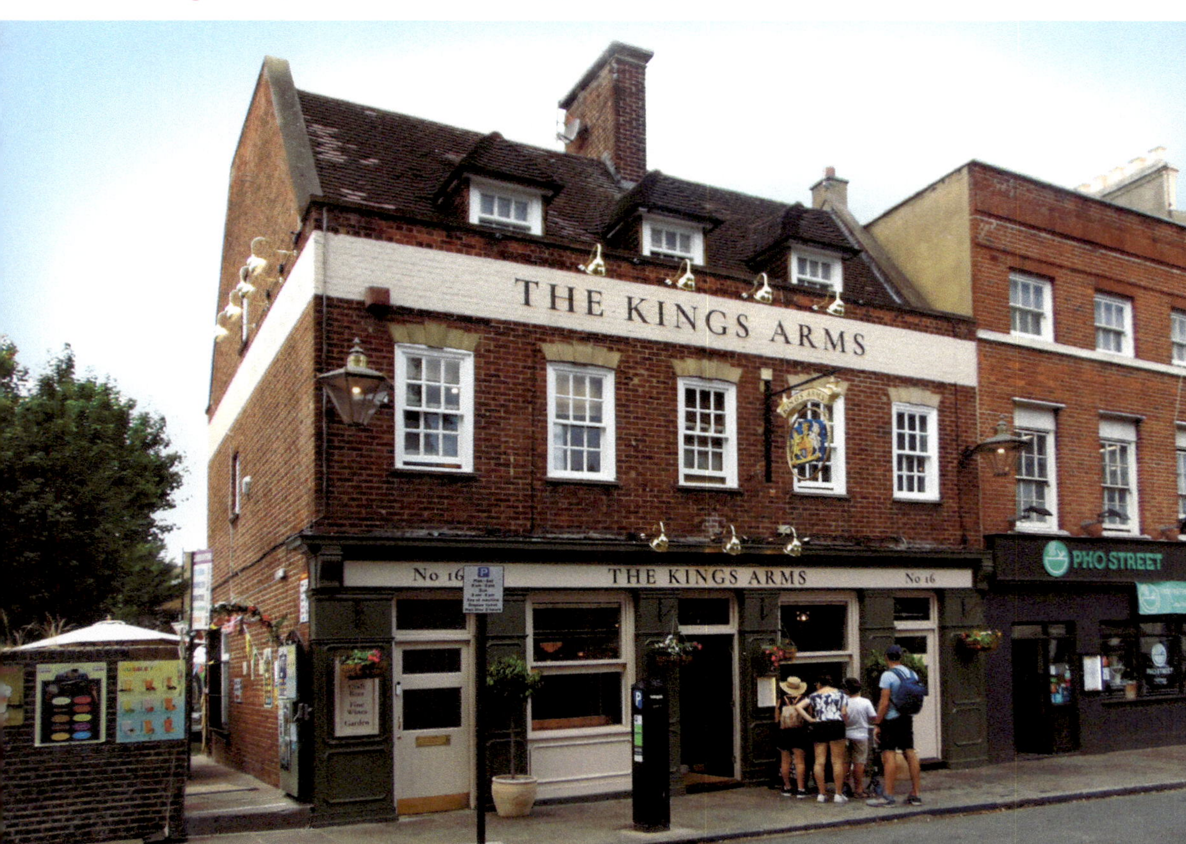

Under the ownership of the Greene King pub chain, the Kings Arms has recently undergone further refurbishment and redecoration, where it is unlikely the pub's drinkers of today will be aware of its local nickname.

THE MITRE, Greenwich High Street

A large spacious building dating to 1830–31, the pub was erected on the site of an eighteenth-century coffee shop, also named the Mitre, where amateur choral group the East Greenwich Madrigal Society met weekly.

The original building burned down in 1829, during a period when much of the slum areas of medieval Greenwich were being cleared and rebuilt. Situated to the south of St Alfege's Church, where Archbishop of Canterbury Alphege (also spelt Alfege) was killed by the Danes in 1012, the Mitre takes its name from the traditional religious ceremonial headwear, dating to at least the eleventh century, worn by Christian bishops and abbots. After the Reformation the mitre headwear went out of fashion in the Church of England, then came back in favour during nineteenth century, around the time the pub was rebuilt.

After the rebuilding, West Greenwich was becoming a notable and fashionable place for wealthy people to live, with coffee houses, restaurants, theatres and shops, and the Mitre was divided into various bars to accommodate the differing class of clientele.

The Mitre after refurbishment in 2022.

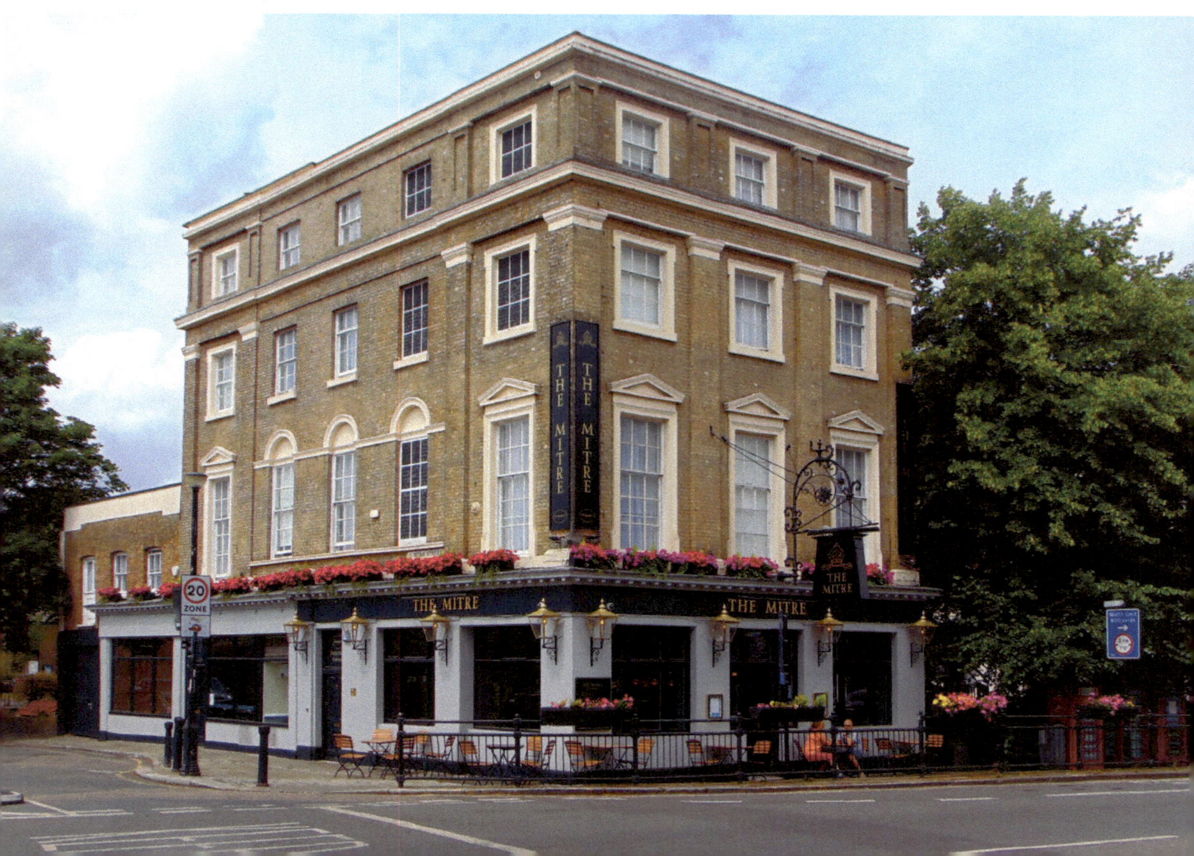

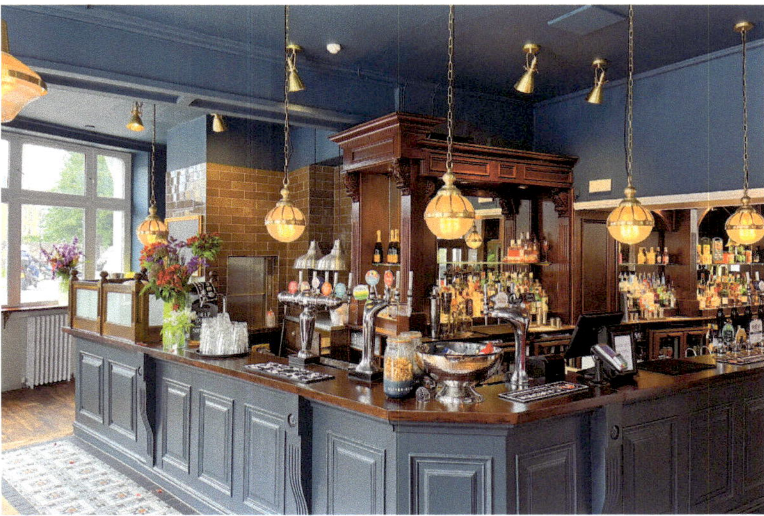

Corner bar of
the Mitre.

The Mitre also offered accommodation over the building's upper three floors for visitors drawn to Greenwich's many attractions.

Badly damaged by bombing to the Mitre's front and first floor during the Second World War, unlike other public houses which were then demolished after suffering such bomb damage, the pub was repaired and reopened. After several refurbishments the individual bars have long since gone, and the pub is now laid out in an open plan style, with a long bar, outside seating areas and a conservatory to the rear. Protected as a Grade II listed building in 1973, for its special architectural and historic interest, the Mitre was then declared a World Heritage Site by UNESCO in 1997.

THE GREENWICH TAVERN, King William Street

Originally named the Gloucester Arms, the present building, erected in 1851, replaced the Gloucester Hotel and Tea Gardens, which completely burned down in a fire that broke out during the night. Attended to first by local parish and Greenwich Hospital firefighting engines, the fire was so fierce they were joined around midnight by West of England and London Fire Brigade engines. The licensee at the time, Andrew Larkin, had fully insured the building, and after the pub was rebuilt, he continued in his role of landlord up until his death in 1863, succeeded by his widow, Elizabeth Larking, who served as licensee for at least five years.

Now part of the Greene King chain, the pub was originally named after Humphrey, Duke of Gloucester, fourth son of Henry IV. The duke was instrumental in shaping Greenwich Park, and the pub is located on a corner opposite St Mary's Park Gates at the south end of King William Street, now King William Walk. Humphrey enclosed 200 acres of land for royal hunting parties after acquiring Old Court, from where the Manor of Greenwich was administered, erecting a fortified tower, Greenwich Castle, at the park's centre, later demolished to build Greenwich Royal Observatory.

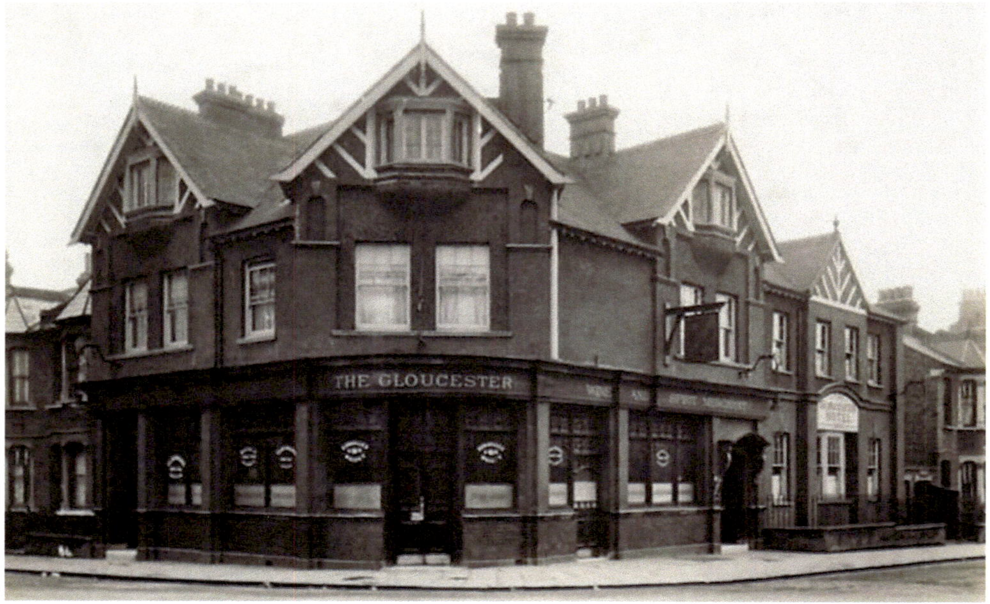

The Gloucester Arms, mid-1900s.

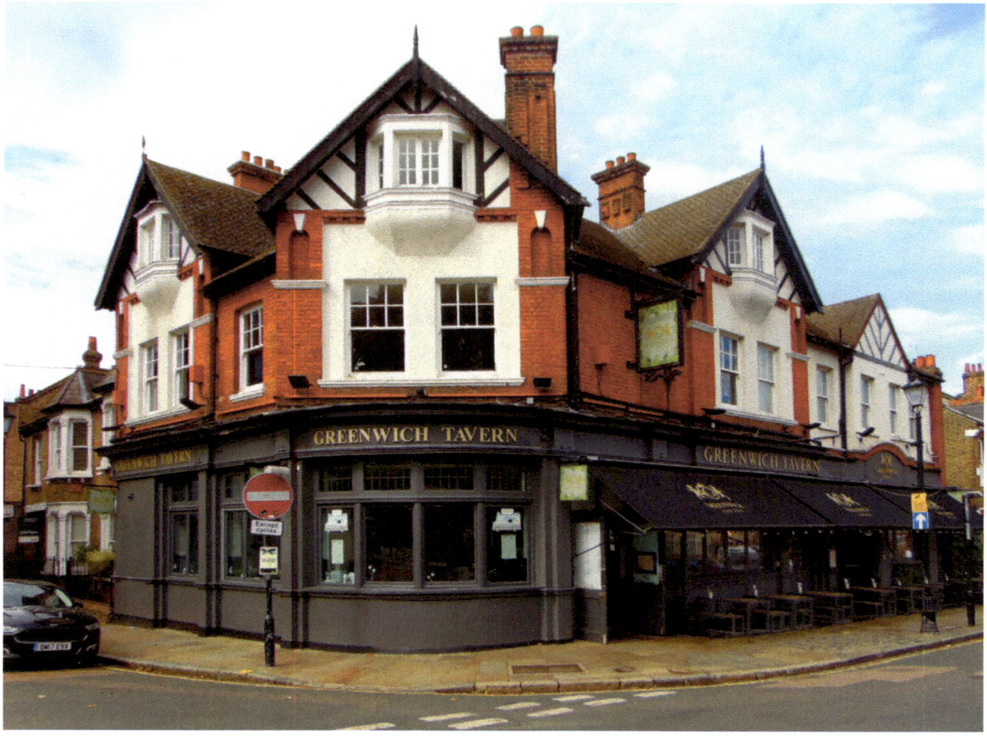

The Greenwich Tavern, 2022.

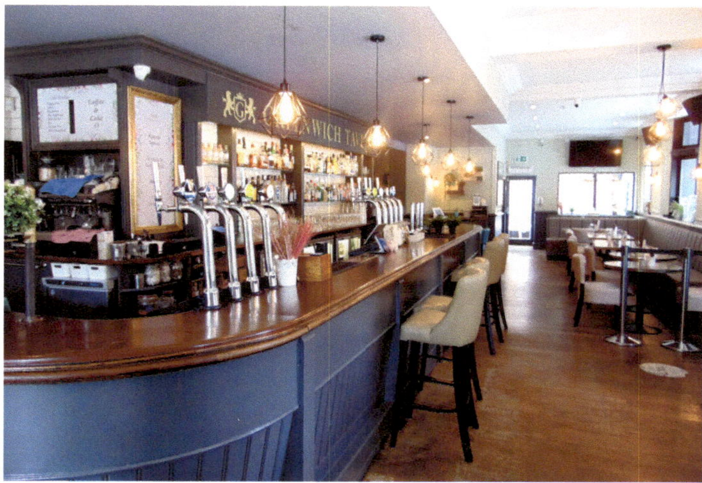

The modern
open bar of the
Greenwich Tavern.

For a majority of the pub's time after the rebuild, the Gloucester served the general local populace, then in the 1980s, for a time, it became a place where clandestine wheelers and dealers of pilfered goods got together to carry out transactions over a pint. During the 1990s, the Gloucester was one of the first pubs to become an accepted meeting place for the gay community.

Renamed the Greenwich Park Bar and Grill, the pub evolved into a popular place to eat and drink at weekends for tourists and families visiting the park, where a row of tables and chairs are set up undercover outside for periods of inclement weather. Although the pub's name changed again, to the Greenwich Tavern, for locals of my age, and older, the pub will always be referred to as the Gloucester.

YE OLDE ROSE & CROWN, Crooms Hill

It is believed that an inn or tavern had occupied the site since the reign of Elizabeth I, the current pub rebuilt in 1888. Originally part of a popular theatre and music hall, today Ye Olde Rose & Crown carries on a theatrical tradition by hosting various evening performances by vibrant and colourful drag artistes.

Ye Olde Rose & Crown became a welcoming destination for the LGBTQ community, along with local residents and tourists, Nathan, the pub's general manager, organising various fun events for charity, quizzes, and bingo nights.

On a prominent corner position of Crooms Hill and Nevada Street, the pub building is enclosed on two sides by Greenwich Theatre, erected on the site of Ye Olde Rose & Crown Music Hall, which then became a theatre, where performers of the day, including Dan Leno, Kitty Fairdale, Arthur Lloyd and Ellen Terry, entertained audiences coming from far and wide.

After the theatre was refurbished as a picture house, and then suffered bomb damage during the Second World War, it was rebuilt around the existing pub with a new main box office entrance erected on Crooms Hill, theatre performances include festive pantomimes, comedies, musicals, and dramas.

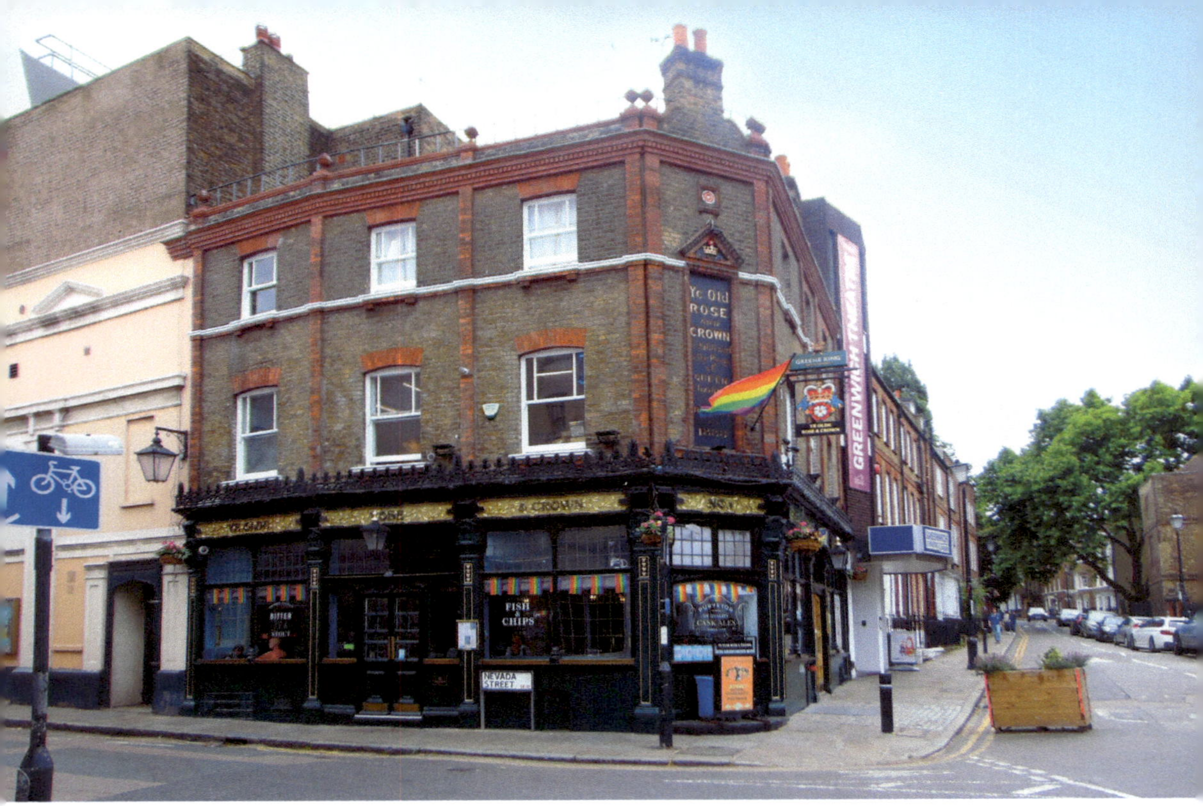

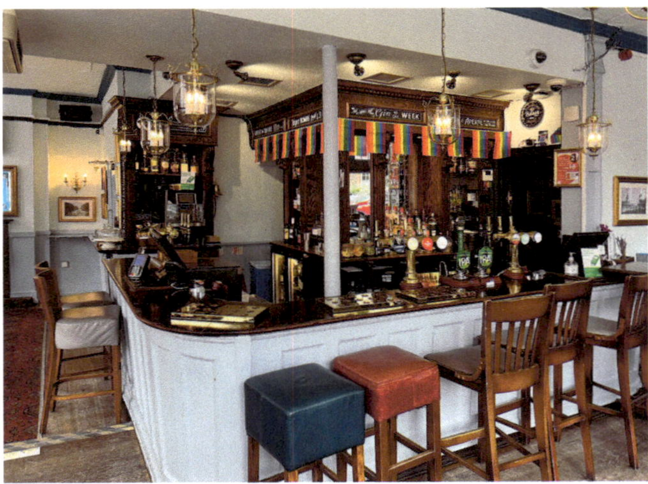

One night in January 2018, just after closing, Ye Olde Rose & Crown became the scene of a real-life drama when three armed robbers burst in through the doors while a member of staff was clearing up at the end of the day. Forced to hand over money from that day's takings, the thieves, one brandishing a gun and another a machete, then made off towards Gloucester Circus, where it was believed a getaway car was waiting, the curtain coming down on the night's performance.

Once tied to Taylor Walker & Co. brewery, Ye Olde Rose and Crown is now another Greenwich Green King pub. The brewery is extremely supportive of LGBTQ community, and the wider community as a whole.

THE LOST HOUR, Greenwich High Road

Occupying a plain-looking, red-brick, two-storey building erected during the early 1950s, The Lost Hour was originally known as The Auctioneer.

Formerly Faulkner's Furniture shop, where my mother once worked in the accounts department, when the shop closed it became Thomas Moore's Auction House, before being refurbished and converted into a pub during the late 1900s called The Auctioneer. This became a favourite place for students to hang out after a day's studying.

After acquired in the early 2000s by the Stonegate Pub Company, now the largest pub chain in the UK, the pub's name was changed to The Lost Hour. Redecorated to attract slightly older groups of clientele, the pub offered a selection of imaginative cocktails and shots, along with traditional beers, wines and spirits, and with the approach of the 2012 London Olympics, Greenwich hosting a variety of the sporting events, The Lost Hour took on the resemblance of a trendy sports bar.

Following refurbishment in 2017, The Lost Hour, spread over two floors, has large-screen monitors showing live sports events, a selection of retro console games available for regulars to play, as well as a pool table. Serving a range of contemporary food and drinks, The Lost Hour, a Cask Marque accredited pub, also offers over thirteen different craft beers, said to be the most available in Greenwich.

The Lost Hour, originally a furniture store.

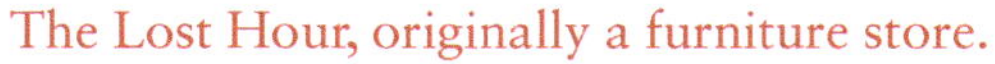

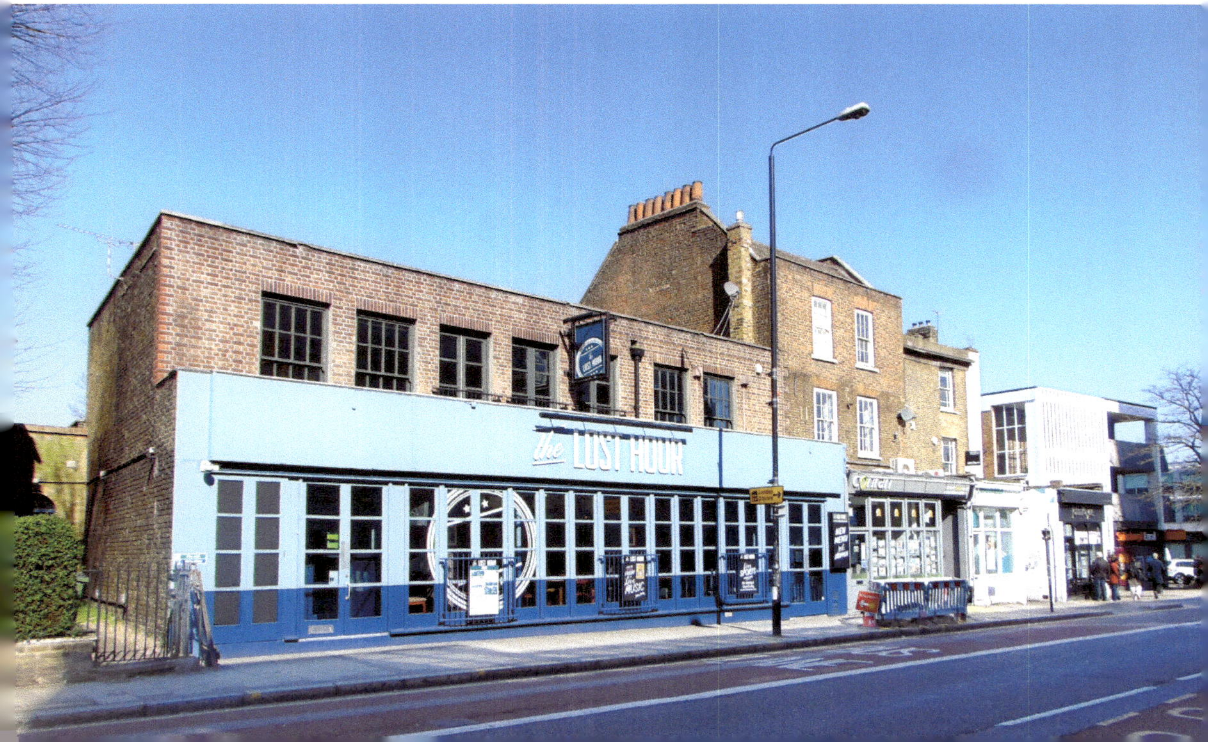

BELUSHI'S, Greenwich High Road

Built in the traditional style of many other large early nineteenth-century public houses located adjacent to Greenwich station, Belushi's was first known as The Prince of Orange, after William III of England who, along with his wife, Queen Mary II, held court at Greenwich during the early period of their reign.

Predating the building of the present Greenwich railway station by some thirty-five years, the licensee at this time, William Robinson, saw an increase in trade, and profits, after the railway line first opened at Greenwich in 1838, being the closest pub to the station, where train passengers took refreshment before their departure and after their arrival.

Towards the end of the Second World War, the Prince of Orange had expanded into the Station Hotel to the rear, to increase its business operations, the pub becoming a popular and successfully profitable establishment. During the late 1970s, The Prince of Orange was one of the pubs my friends and I would meet up specifically to have a few games of bar billiards before heading off to watch the club we support, Charlton Athletic, play at home on a Saturday.

In the late 1900s, after a rise in popularity of experimental London pub theatre performances, part of The Prince of Orange was converted to accommodate the sixty-two-seater Greenwich Studio Theatre, afterwards known as the Prince Theatre, where year round professional classic and modern dramas were performed to much critical acclaim.

Belushi's and St Christopher's Inn.

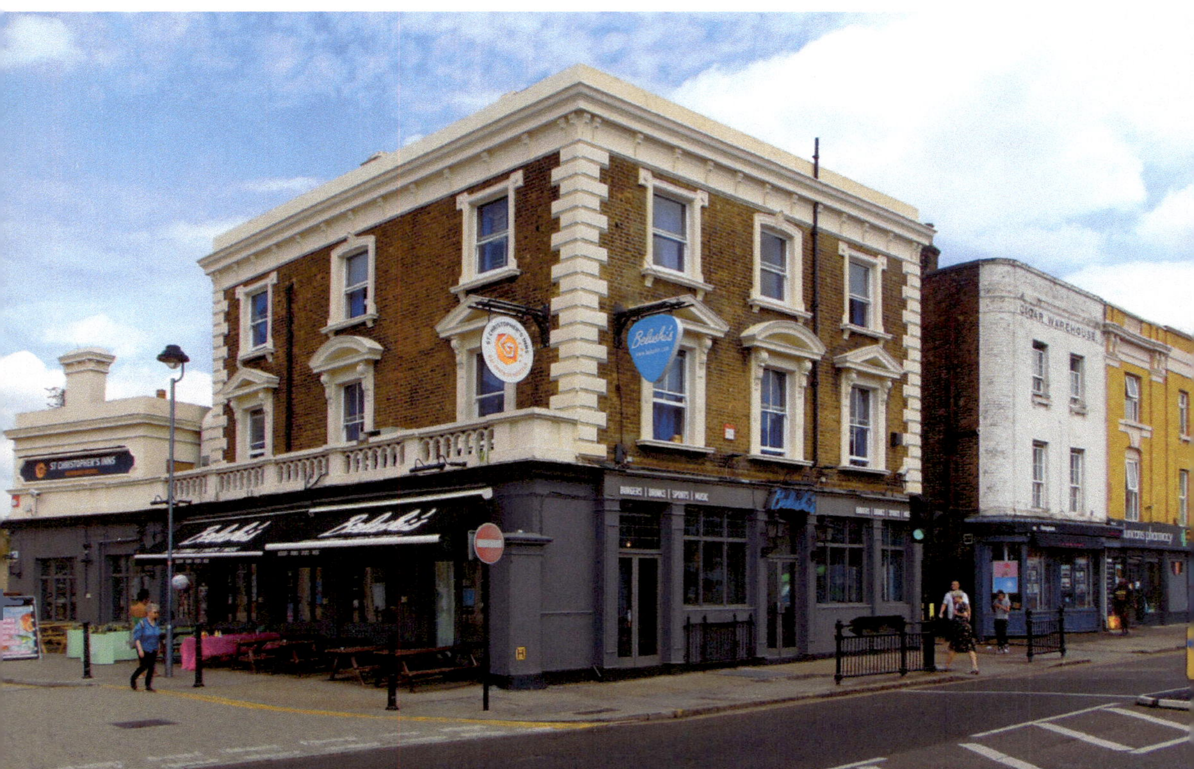

When Interpub took over The Prince of Orange in 2000, the theatre was closed to make way for a backpacker hostel, the pub changing its name to St Christopher's Inn. Part of a group of hostels run under the title of St Christopher's Inns, by parent company Beds and Bars, the pub was then renamed Belushi's, one of several in the chain, undergoing a complete refurbishment in 2018. The pub, now open plan, serves food and drink to a wide range of clientele, vacationers and commuters, tourists, locals and, of course, backpackers.

THE NORTH POLE, Greenwich High Road

Located the furthest west within the parish boundary, away from the main tourist hub of the town centre, the North Pole is another one of Greenwich's large pubs built during the early nineteenth century on a corner block. The pub is believed to have been erected on the site of an earlier public house.

Although Greenwich had associations with nineteenth-century Arctic and Antarctic maritime exploration and navigation, the origin of the pub's name, North Pole, has been lost over the passage of time, just like many of those first explorers setting out to those frozen terrains, lost, never to return.

The North Pole, last pub west of the Meridian Line.

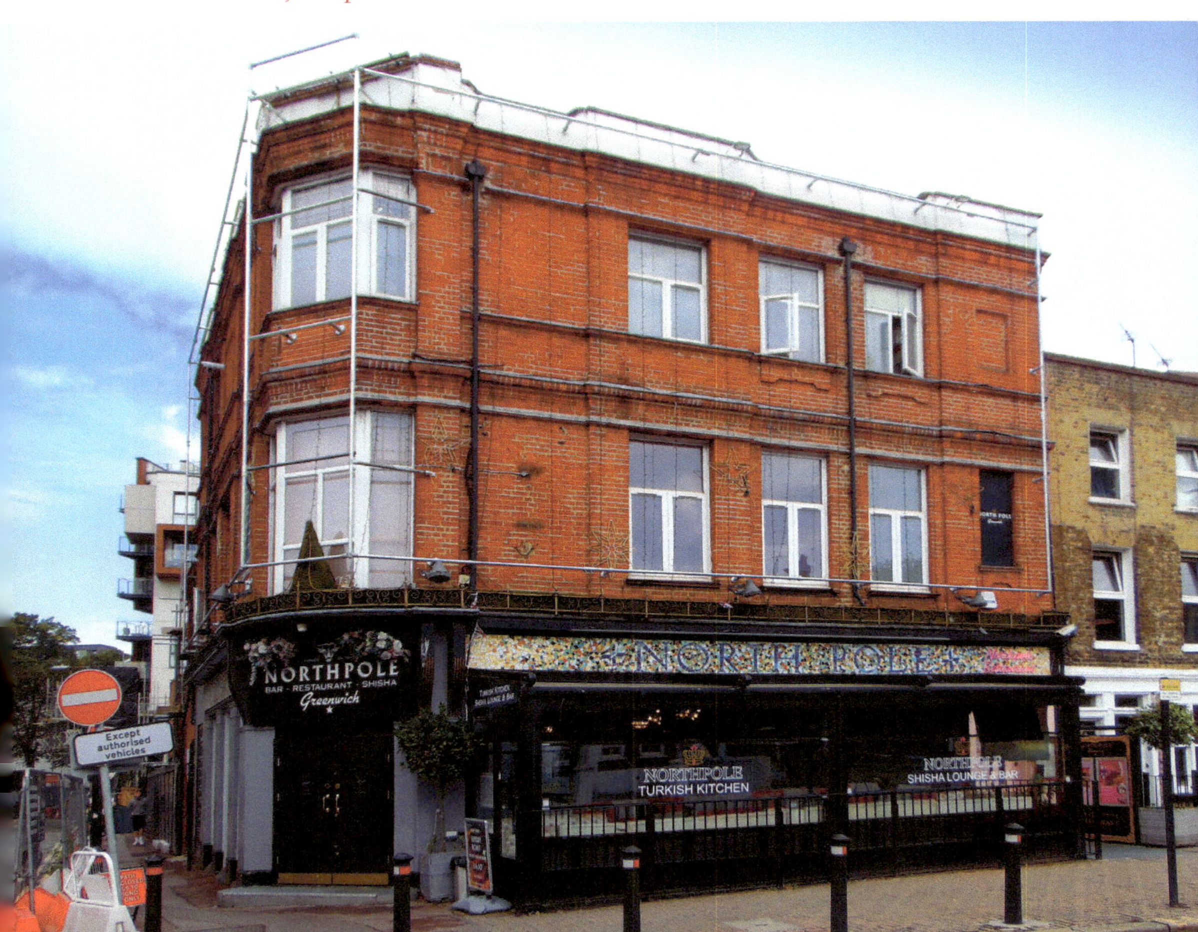

Situated on the corner of Greenwich Road (now Greenwich High Road) and Norman Road, the North Pole was one of several pubs once located on the route from Greenwich to Deptford, just east of Deptford Creek, a thriving ancient waterway lined on each bank by local industries, workshops, wharfs, and yards, the labourers and workers taking refreshment in these pubs at the end of their days work, including the North Pole, usually frequented by those working at the adjacent LCC Sewerage Pumping station.

By the late 1900s, with the closure of a majority of West Greenwich workplaces resulting in a reduction of the once large labour force, many of the pubs in the area lost custom, and unable to make ends meet, eventually closed. The North Pole, however, is one of a few pubs to have survived in the former industrial area of West Greenwich. Continuing with its working-class traditions up into the early 2000s, you could still find locals playing darts and cribbage, a popular card game played in taverns and beerhouses since the mid-eighteenth century. The North Pole then began holding popular and well-attended lively Sunday jazz sessions.

Under the ownership of the Zinnureyin family, the North Pole was then refurbished and converted into a contemporary bar and restaurant venue, with a nightclub in the basement named the South Pole, aiming to attract a more fashionable assembly of clientele.

The bright and lavishly decorated bar of the North Pole.

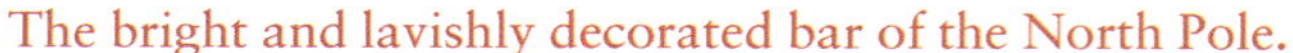

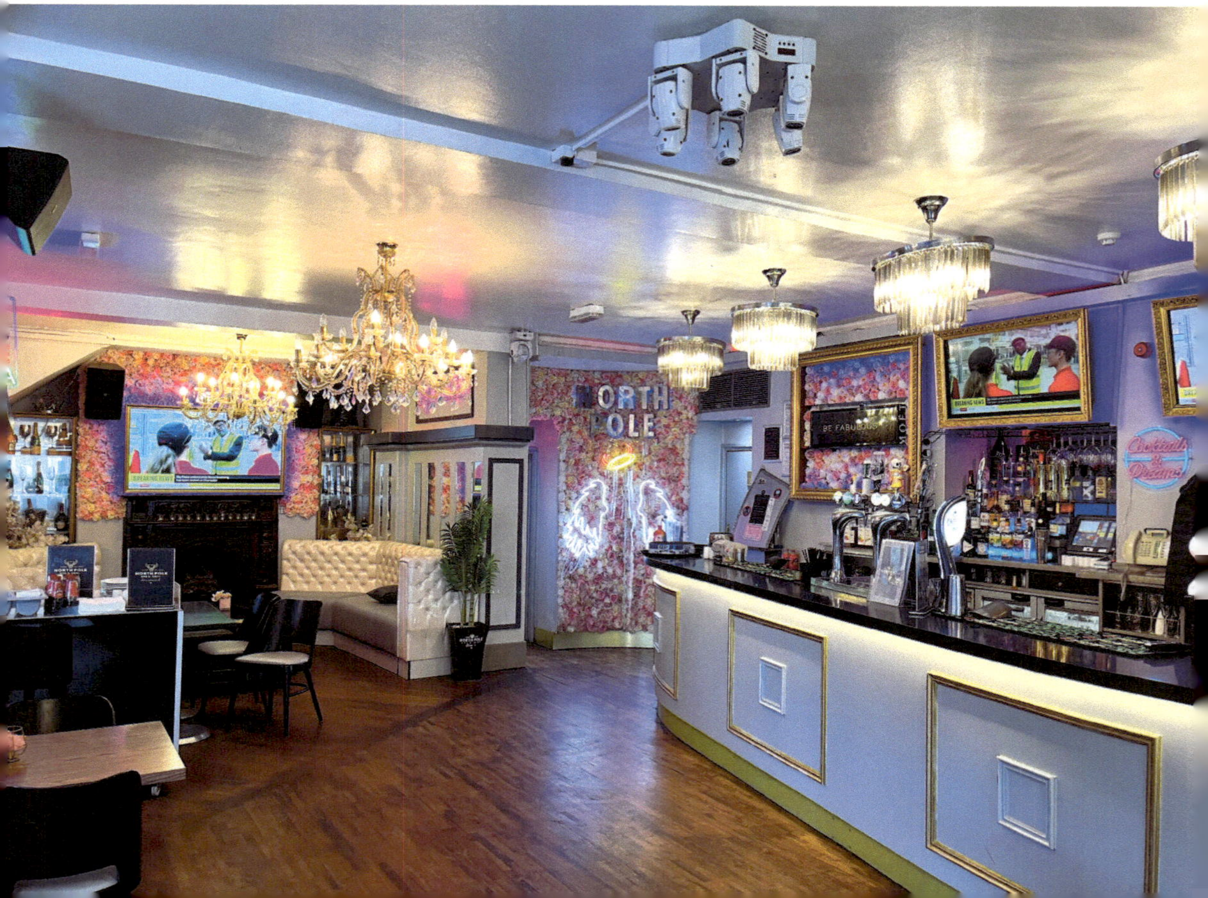

After a series of incidents at the pub, bar brawls and drug taking, the North Pole was threatened with closure, which resulted in the owners at the time closing the nightclub and changing the pub's business model to a more up market, smart gastropub environment. The North Pole now attracts a clientele made up of new residents moving into an area undergoing regeneration, the industrial landscape replaced by modern apartments and leisure facilities.

THE MORDEN ARMS, Brand Street

Named after Sir John Morden, a wealthy merchant and philanthropist who founded a home for retired merchants at Blackheath, the Morden Arms was built on the corner of Brand Street and Circus Street in the early 1840s.

A few years after opening, in February 1846, during a coroner's inquest held at the pub into the death of a child, a shocking case of incest was uncovered. William Richardson, assistant to the Royal Observatory's Astronomer Royal, appeared at the inquest after the remains of a child were discovered buried in his garden.

During investigation it was reveal Richardson had been carrying out an incestuous relationship with his daughter, who gave birth to a son, the child dying ten days later, Richardson secretly disposing of the baby's body in the garden.

The Morden Arms, unremarkable from the outside.

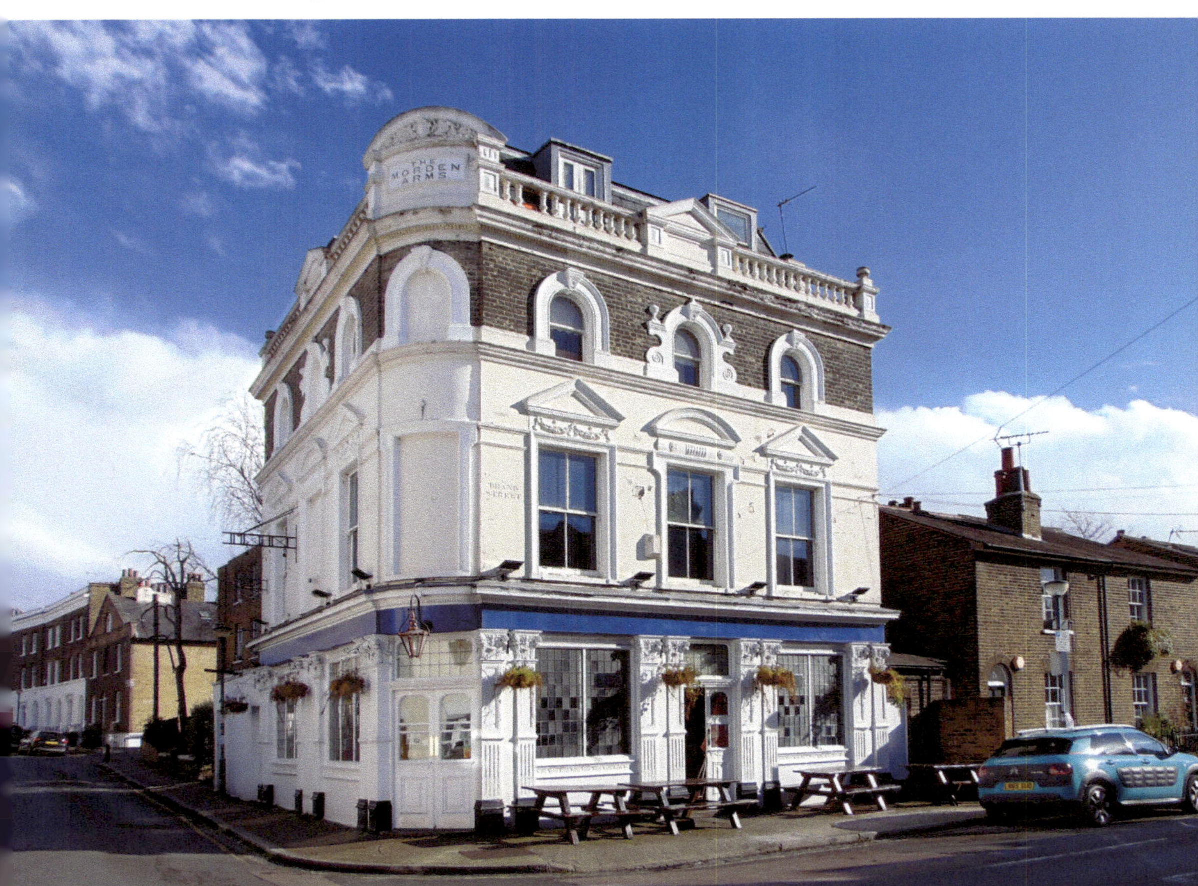

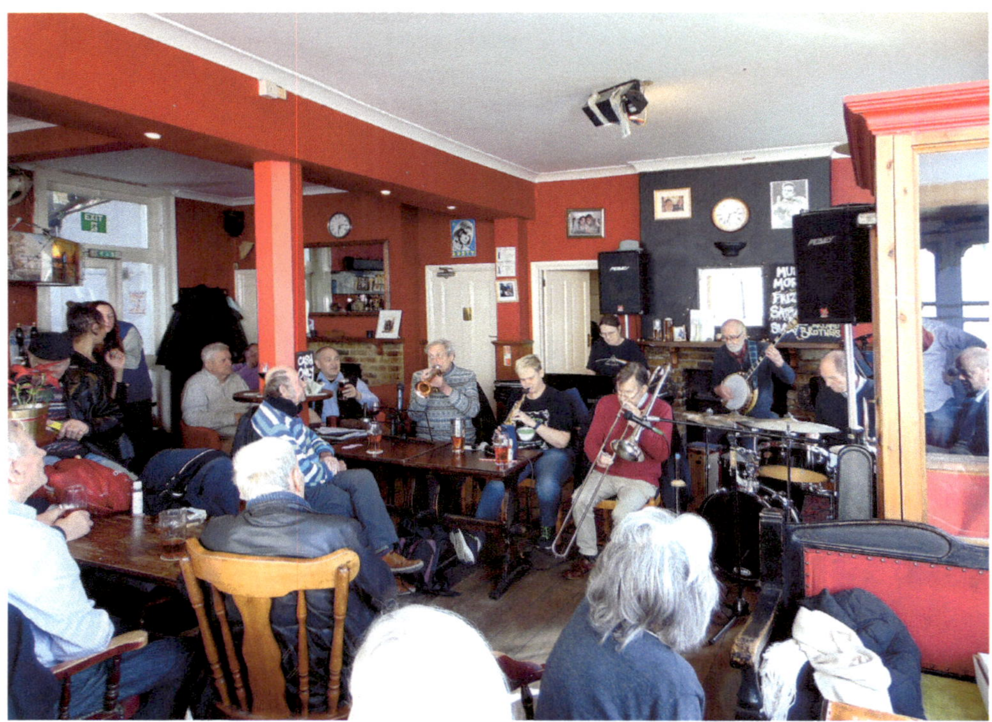

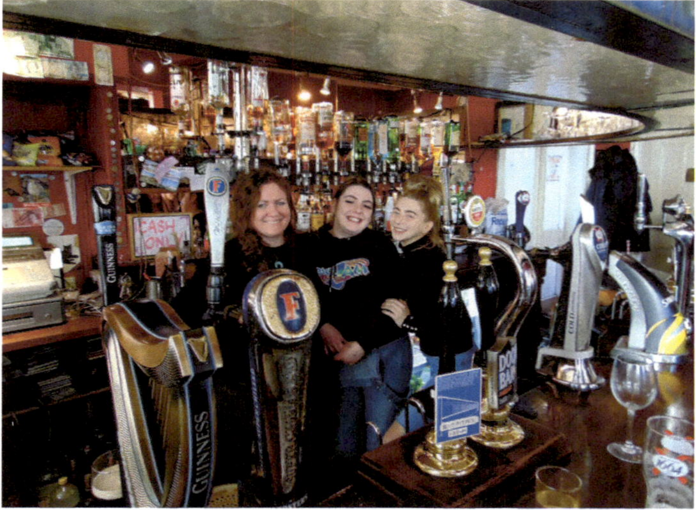

Above: The Modern Arms jazz session – lively on the inside.

Left: Girls behind the Morden Arms bar, Hannah, Angalene and Katie.

Although incest was not a criminal offence at this time, Richardson was found guilty of murder, when forensic tests showed that the child had most likely died by arsenic poisoning. Although Richardson and his daughter were sent to appear at the Old Bailey, due to lack of conclusive evidence, both father and daughter were acquitted of murder, the incident a much talked about event among the pub's regulars well into the late 1800s.

Tucked away on a side street, the outward appearance of the Morden Arms gives an impression of just another unassuming boozer. However, on entering you will find a large open space with a 'shabby chic' interior and a long traditional-style bar running along the rear of the pub, where friendly bar staff are ready to serve you.

A one-time Courage tied pub, the Morden Arms is now independently run, with a clientele made up from an assembly of locals and music lovers of all ages, some who travel from far and wide to attend regular live open-mic jazz sessions and music nights while having a few drinks in the pubs vibrant and hospitable surroundings.

THE RICHARD I, Royal Hill

Situated in a row of randomly designed early nineteenth-century terraced houses, The Ricard I was believed to have originated as a wine and beerhouse, a time during the 1830s when for a fee payable to the local excise officer anyone was permitted to brew and sell beer. The excise licence would have stated whether the beer could be consumed on the premises, or sold off-sales only, to be consumed in the home.

The Richard I, with the former Fox & Hounds pub to the left.

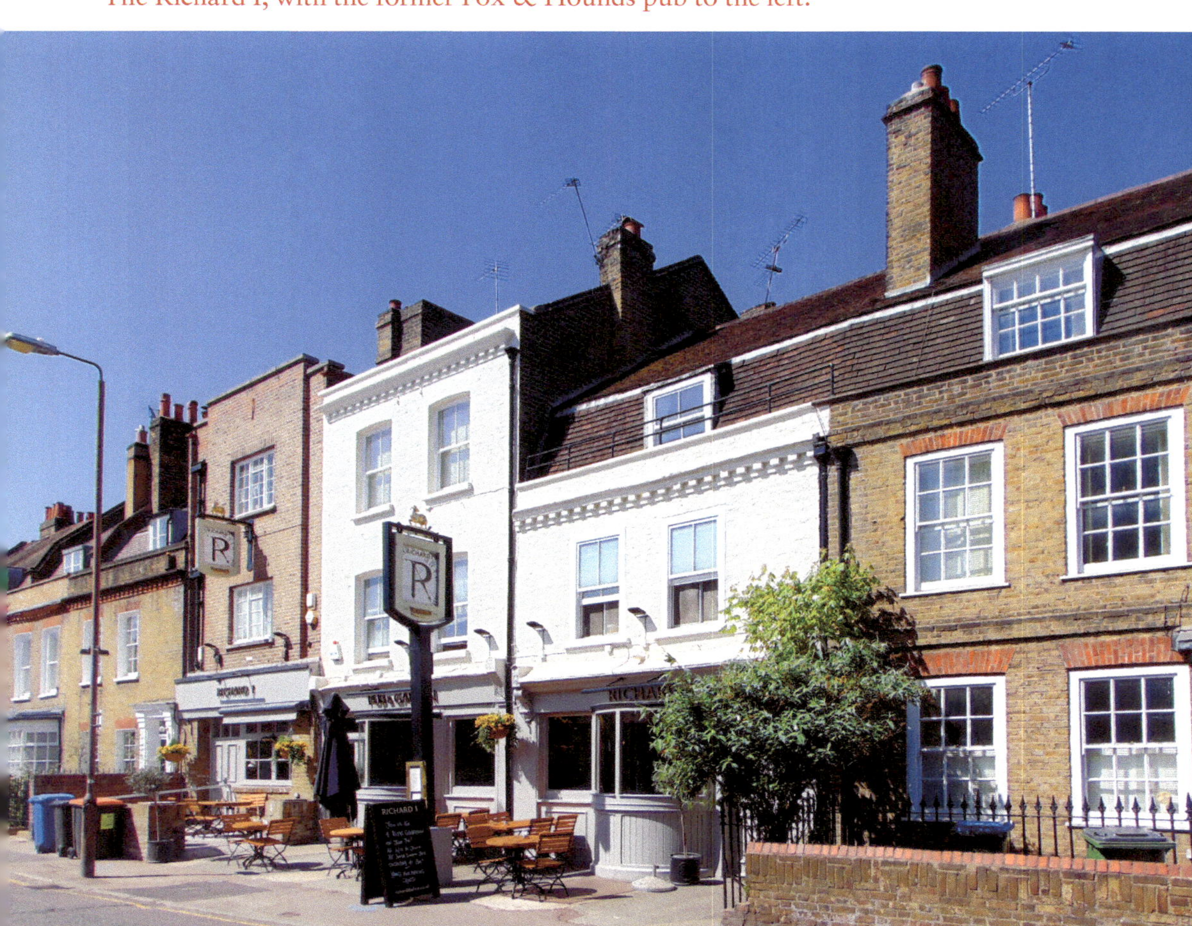

A majority of the buildings on this stretch of Royal Hill, once a medieval route known as Gang Lane, were erected as part a development carried out by Victorian builder Robert Royal, from where the road acquired its new name.

Towards the end of the 1800s, the beerhouse was known as the Richard I, named after the twelfth-century King of England Richard the Lionheart. The pub was situated next door to another beerhouse, The Fox and Hounds.

Although there is no recognised historic connection between Richard I and Greenwich, the king would have passed through the manor, close to Gang Lane, travelling to and from the southern coast of England during crusades to the Holy Land.

Without a full licence, the Richard I continued as a beerhouse going into the 1900s. The owner then acquired an adjacent property to expand the pub's premises. One became the saloon bar and the other a public bar.

Taken over by Ipswich based Toollmache Brewery, the brewery then merged with Cobbold Co. to become Tolly Cobbold Brewery. The Richard I became known by locals as the Tolly House, and for many years displayed this name on the pub's outside signage.

Under the ownership of Youngs, in 2022, the Richard I expanded into premises of the old Fox and Hounds after its closure, the neighbouring pub then going by the name of the Greenwich Union, run by Meantime Brewery.

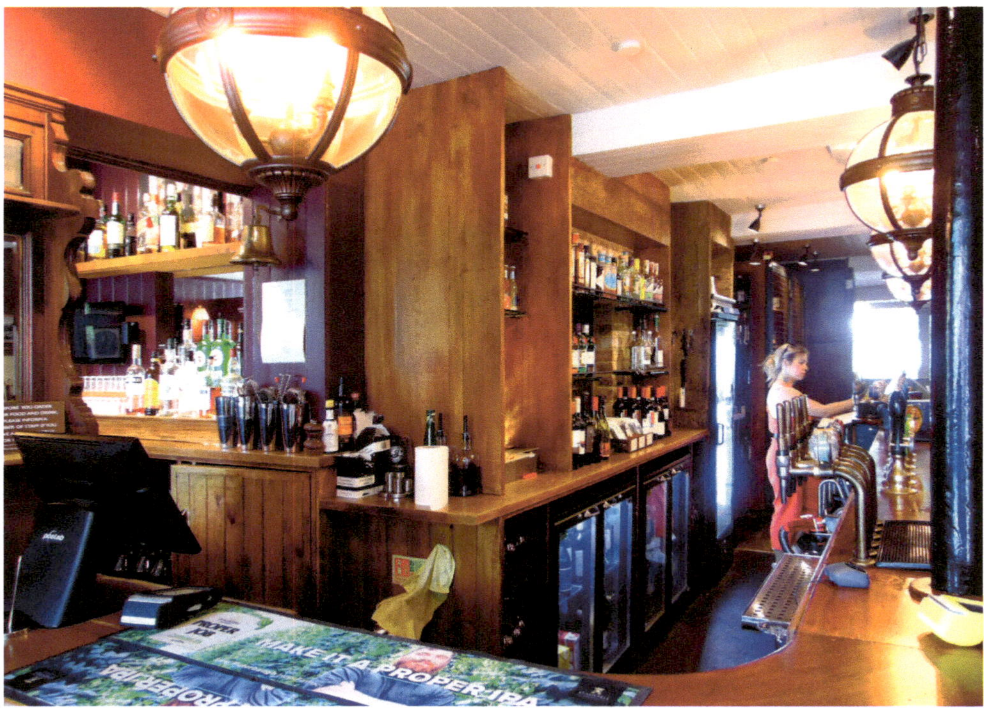

Main bar of Richard I after refurbishment in 2022.

THE PRINCE OF GREENWICH, Royal Hill

Formerly known as The Prince Albert, the pub was built during the reign of Queen Victoria and named after her husband Albert, Prince Consort. As with many pubs built during this period, located amongst terraced houses, the pub was mainly used by local residents. However, after taken over by much travelled Sicilian born Pietro La Rosa and his wife Paola in 2015, the pub, renamed The Prince of Greenwich, has now become a place to visit, people travelling from far and wide, not only to dine and have a drink, but also to see the amazing array of artifacts on display.

Known affectionately as the museum-pub, the interior of The Prince of Greenwich is adorned with various objets d'art and intriguing exhibits, including a sperm whale jaw bone, rhino head, framed images of famous jazz singers, decorative chinaware, and ancient and contemporary carvings and sculptures, which are only a few of the items on show, a majority collected during Pietro's global journeys.

The pub's décor and furnishings included pianos, chaise longues, barber chairs and varied ornate sets of tables and chairs, reflecting a wide-ranging mix of styles and periods, all set out over the ground floor bar areas, and throughout the upstairs rooms and dining area.

The Prince of Greenwich, the museum pub.

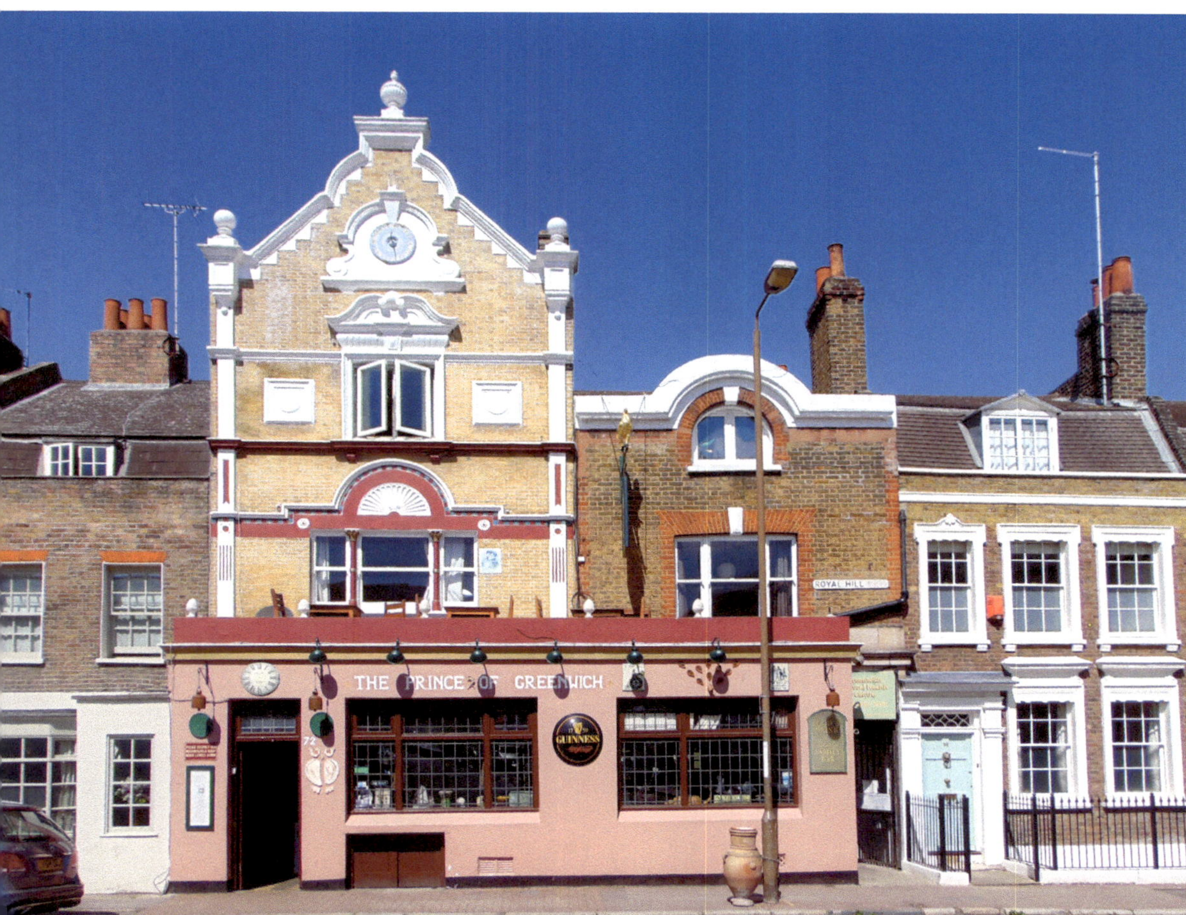

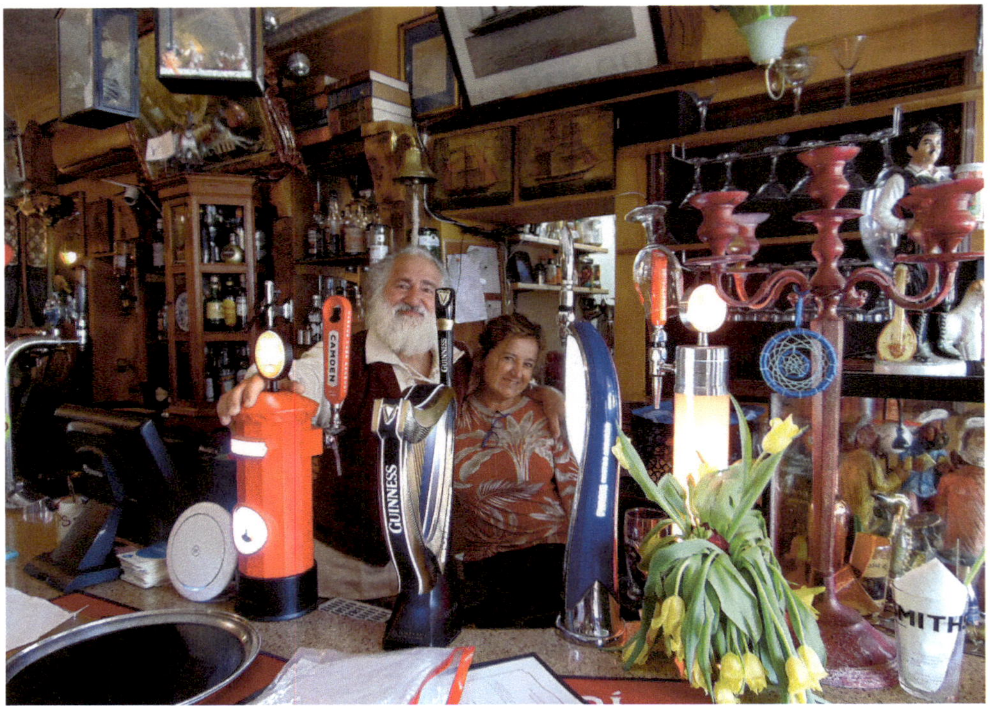

The Prince of Greenwich proprietors Pietro and Paola La Rosa.

Serving a selection of creative home-cooked Mediterranean themed dishes during the week, at weekends, those drinking and dining in the unique surroundings of The Prince of Greenwich are also entertained by bands performing live music sessions.

THE ASHBURNHAM ARMS, Ashburnham Grove

Situated at the heart of the Ashburnham Triangle, a small historical conservation area bounded by three throughfares, Greenwich South Street, Blackheath Road, and Greenwich High Road, the Ashburnham Arms was built at the triangle's centre during the mid-1800s, part of an important residential development consisting of around nine streets and several cul-de-sacs. The land was owned by wealthy entrepreneur John Ashburnham, descendent of the Ashburnham family from East Sussex, who acquired the land from an inheritance, the pub displaying the family's coat of arms on the swing-board signage outside.

Positioned at the end of a row of stuccoed terraced properties, the pub is close to the birthplace of journalist, author, film scriptwriter and thriller writer Edgar Wallace, born in a house on Ashburnham Grove in 1875. Wallace mentioned Ashburnham and his adoption at nine days old in his autobiography, *People*.

Set back on that same road where Wallace was born, the Ashburnham Arms has a large-terraced patio to the front, and garden to the rear with a charming conservatory area. When the pub was built, Greenwich was still part of Kent, the Ashburnham Arms continuing a link with the county through the pub's brewery, Kent based Shepherd Neame.

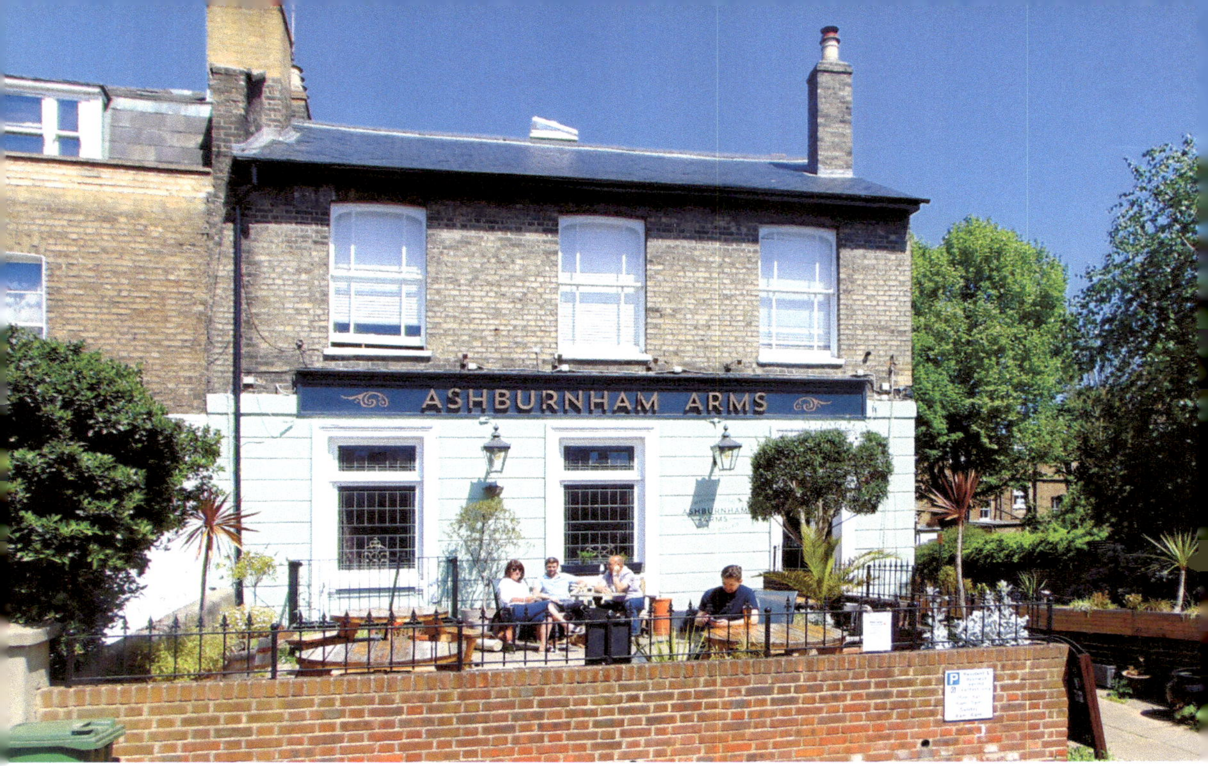

Above: The Ashburnham Arms has ties to Kent and Sussex.

Below: Enclosed beer garden of the Ashburnham Arms.

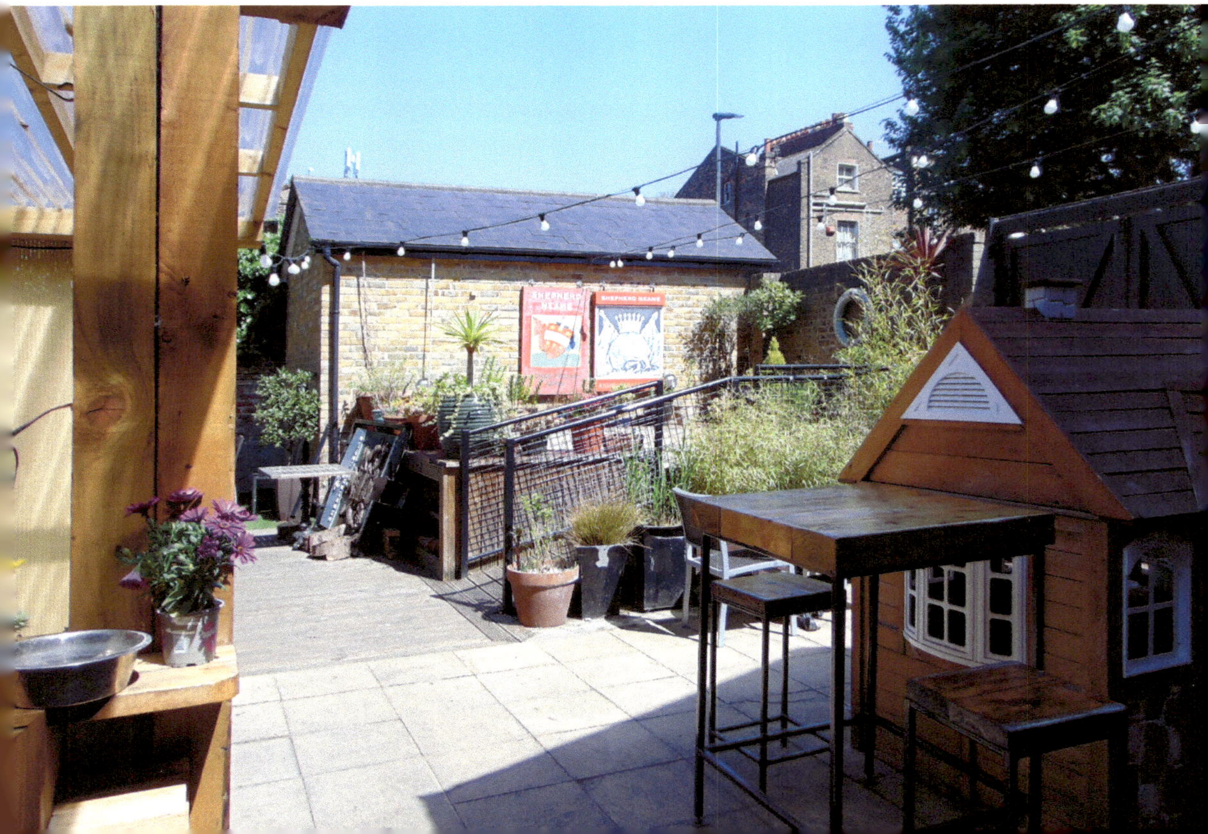

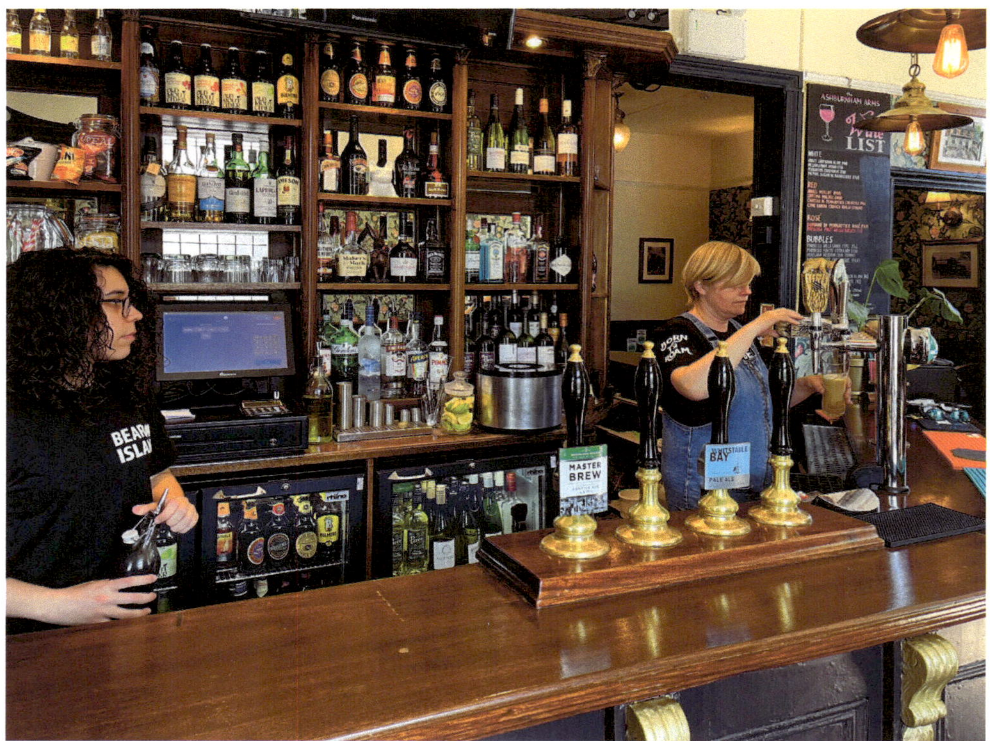

Giulia, senior bartender of the Ashburnham Arms, and Pepinai, manager since 2017.

The Ashburnham Arms provides a comfortable retreat away from the tourist centre of Greenwich, reducing the gap between a traditional local and contemporary modern pub, serving long-established beers and home-cooked pub food, served in hospitable and friendly surroundings of the pub's bars.

THE GUILDFORD ARMS, Guildford Grove

Built in 1796, the Guildford Arms was first commissioned as a residential dwelling by Royal Navy Captain Abraham Reed, who died at sea. The handsome Regency-styled property was then sold on by his widow to practising surgeon John R. Ryder. On Ryder's death in 1806, the house was acquired by two surgeons, and was subsequently purchased by Deptford brewer John Norfolk for use as an alehouse, where he was only licensed to sell his beer.

On application to sell wines and spirits by licensee Isaac Toynbee in 1809, the alehouse was then registered as the Guildford Arms, named after Sir Henry Guildford, resident of Greenwich during the mid-1500s, and controller of Henry VIII's Royal Household at Greenwich Palace.

After a succession of innkeepers, the Guildford Arms came under sole ownership of the Peckham Brewery in 1872, and during the early 1900s was acquired by Charrington & Co. of Mile End.

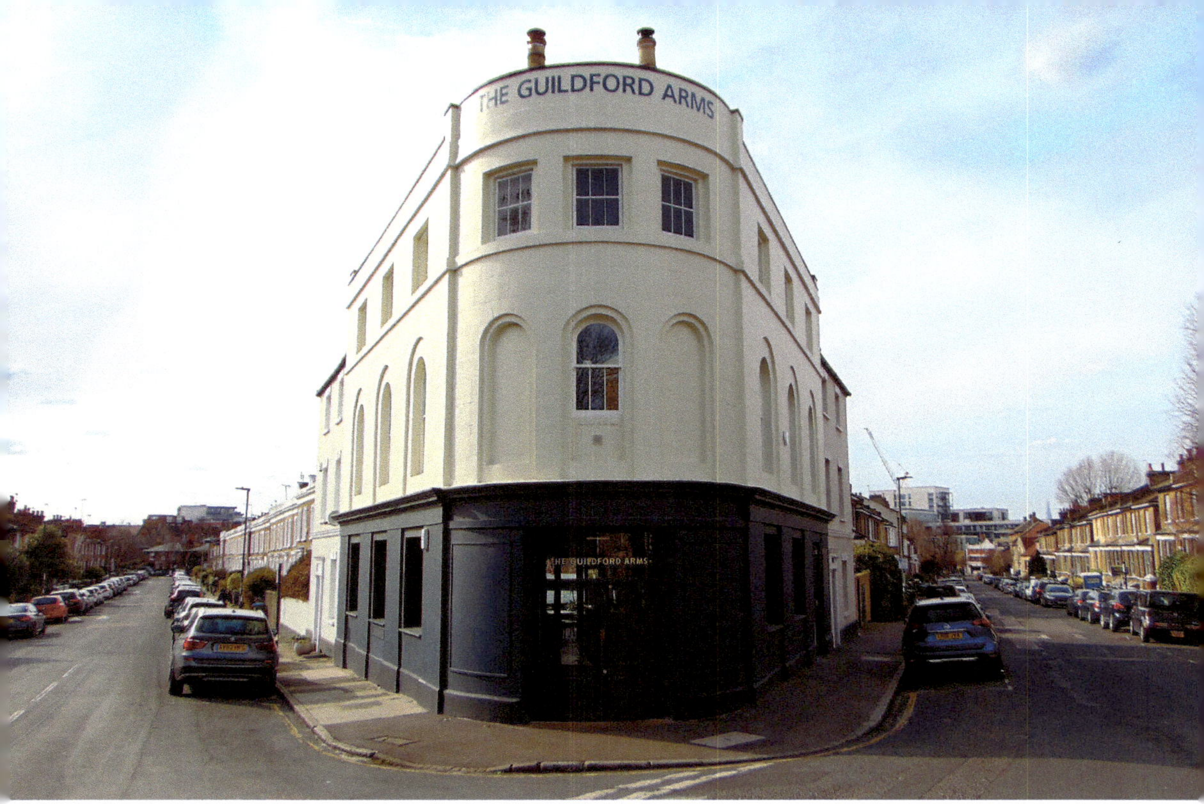

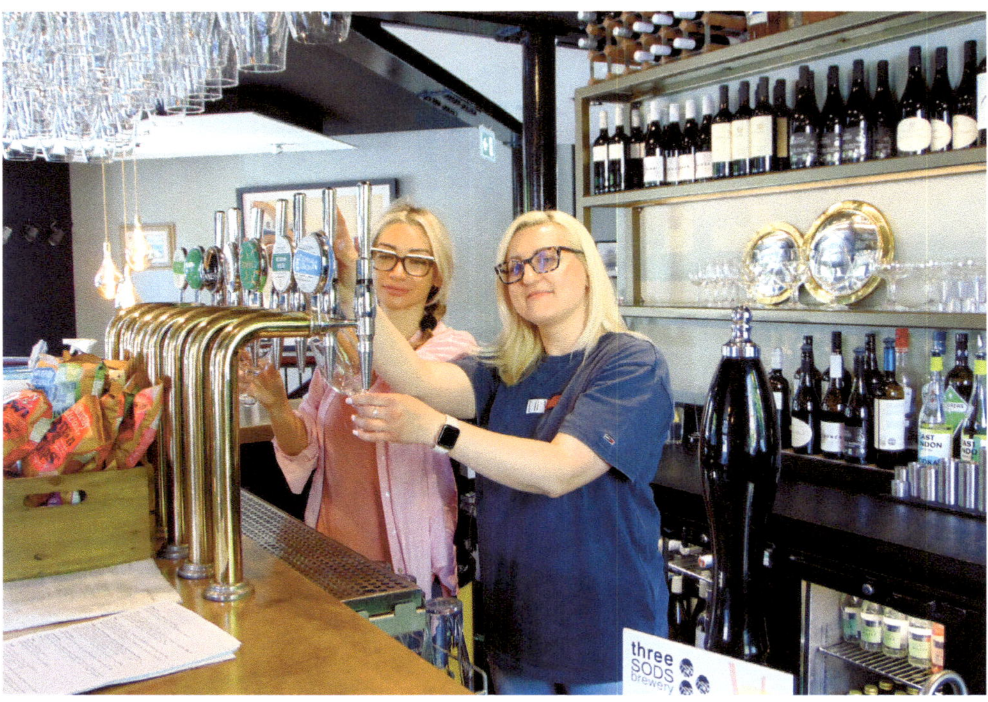

Above: The Guildford Arms, toward the south of the parish.

Below: The Guildford Arms manager Folina and supervisor Ewelina.

Refurbished in 2009, the listed Guildford Arms became more predominantly food orientated for fine dining, named the London Dining Pub of the Year 2018 by the Good Pubs Guide. The pub serves a wide variety of quality seasonal British dishes from the kitchen, built around a charcoal grill and induction slider, to customers in the pub's contemporary designed restaurant, bar and a dining area overlooking an impressively landscaped sunken garden.

The garden is furnished with tables and chairs where you can relax on a summer's day with a wine, cocktail, beer or even a traditional ale.

THE GRADUATE, Blackheath Road

Situated on the corner of Blackheath Road and Greenwich South Street, the Graduate, formerly the Coach & Horses, is one of the few pubs that has been refurbished and re-established. Irish themed, the pub now offers drinkers, along with beer, pool tables, a dart board and several large screens showing sport.

Although the first recorded landlord dates to the early 1800s, the existing building was erected towards the late nineteenth century. However, as its name and location suggests, the original pub was once a staging post for coaches travelling the Old Dover Road.

The Graduate.

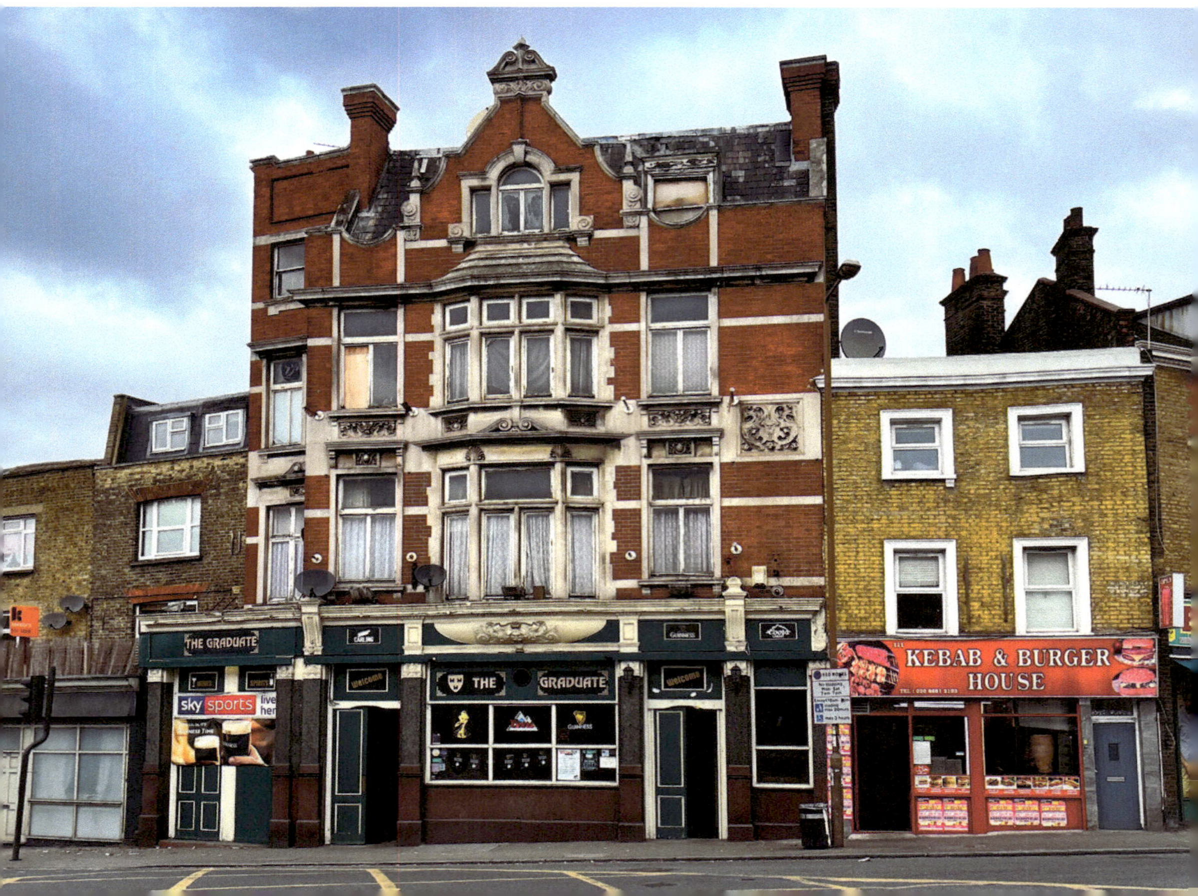

During the mid-1800s, the Coach & Horses would have been frequented by workers at John Penn & Sons marine steam engine manufacturers opposite. Renamed the Graduate in 2000, pub customers now come from a wide section of the local community.

GEORGE & DRAGON, Blackheath Hill

Rebuilt in 1890, the address of the original George & Dragon was on Conduit Vale, the road named after one of several brick-built water conduits located across the south of Greenwich and Blackheath. The only Greenwich pub to bear the name, George & Dragon had become a much sort after title for inns and taverns during the reign of Edward III, when the king chose St George as the patron saint of England, and the name continued to be popular well into the nineteenth century, around the time the first pub was built.

Like many others in the vicinity, the George & Dragon would have once served beer to workers employed in local industries. Today however, the pub, going through a refit and restoration, is now an established contemporary late night gay cabaret bar, with karaoke evenings and a variety of drag acts performing at weekends and on special occasions throughout the year.

The George & Dragon.

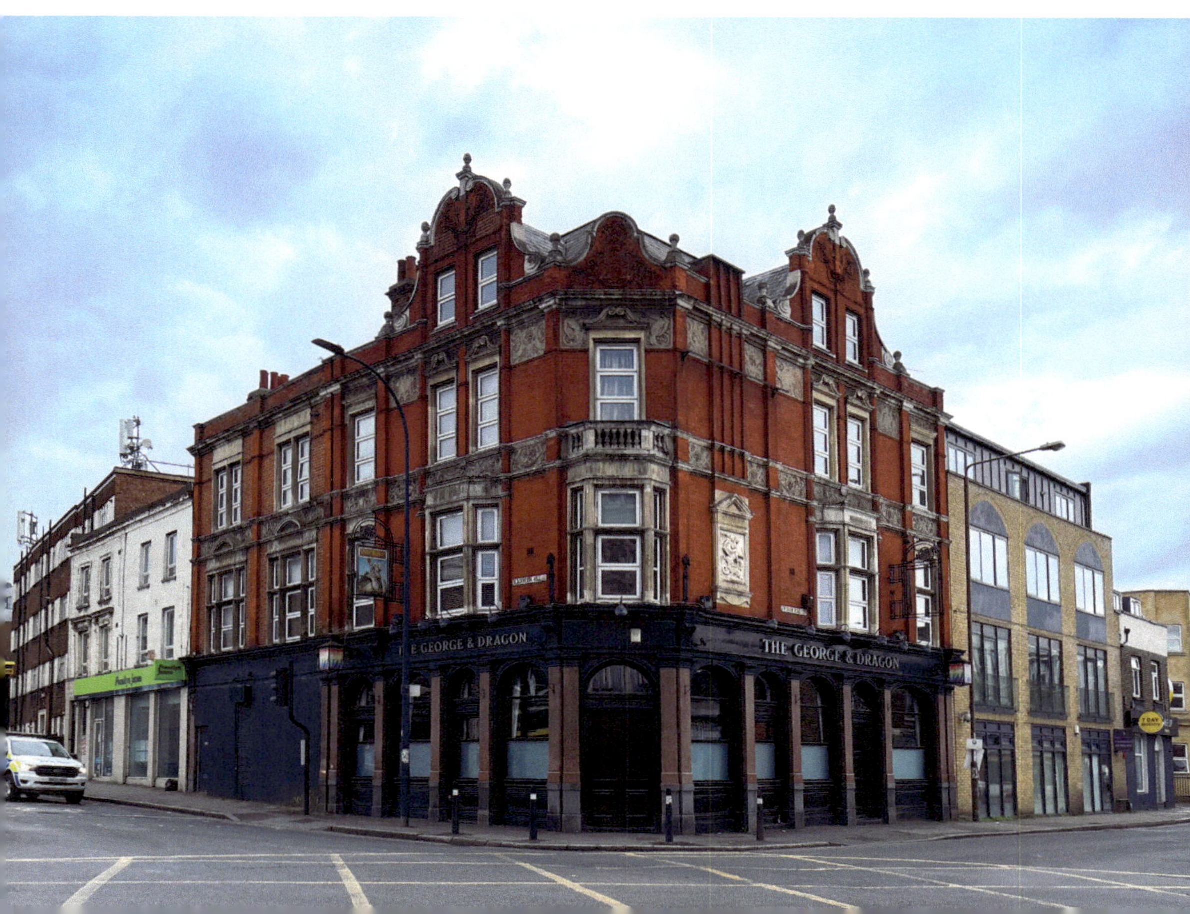

4

East Greenwich

By the late 1800s, much of Greenwich Marsh, previously a large area of marshland and grazing meadows, was owned by charities, with parcels leased to tenants who then sub-let them for development by various industries, and where homes were built on vacant pockets of the marsh. Residential properties were also built to the east from the Meridian Line, south of the Thames, both areas accommodating the industrial and riverside workforce.

The British Queen, Trafalgar Road, now a turf accountants.

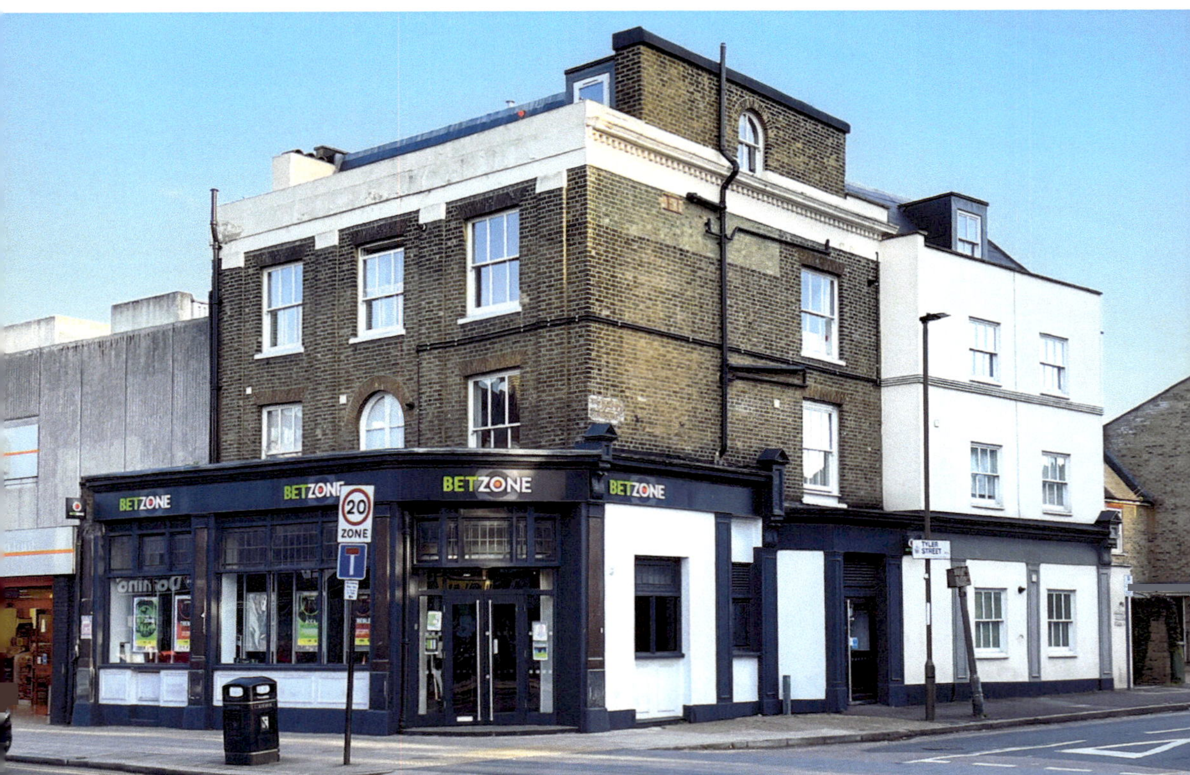

Along with these homes, public houses were also erected to provide sustenance for the workers and their families. Gradually, however, as working practices changed and many industries began to close, these pubs began to lose custom, many eventually closing.

Between the mid-1800s to mid-1900s, there were approximately sixteen public houses, each with their own distinctive character, on the main thoroughfare running through East Greenwich (Woolwich Road and Trafalgar Road) from the parish boundary in the east, to the Meridian Line, which divides the riverside town centrally. At the time of writing existing pubs along this route number just five.

At the end of the Second World War, during a period of redevelopment, many East Greenwich pubs, some damaged during bombing raids, were demolished and replaced by new residential and retail properties. Others however, were forced to close, unable to survive financially during a change in the local communities social demographics.

Some long-time residents of Greenwich can still recall the names of many of those lost post-war pubs, a few old enough to remember having a drink in some, including a number which have closed within the past twenty years, such as British Queen, Old Friends, Duke of Wellington, and Victoria.

The Duke of Wellington, closed in the late 1900s and converted into flats.

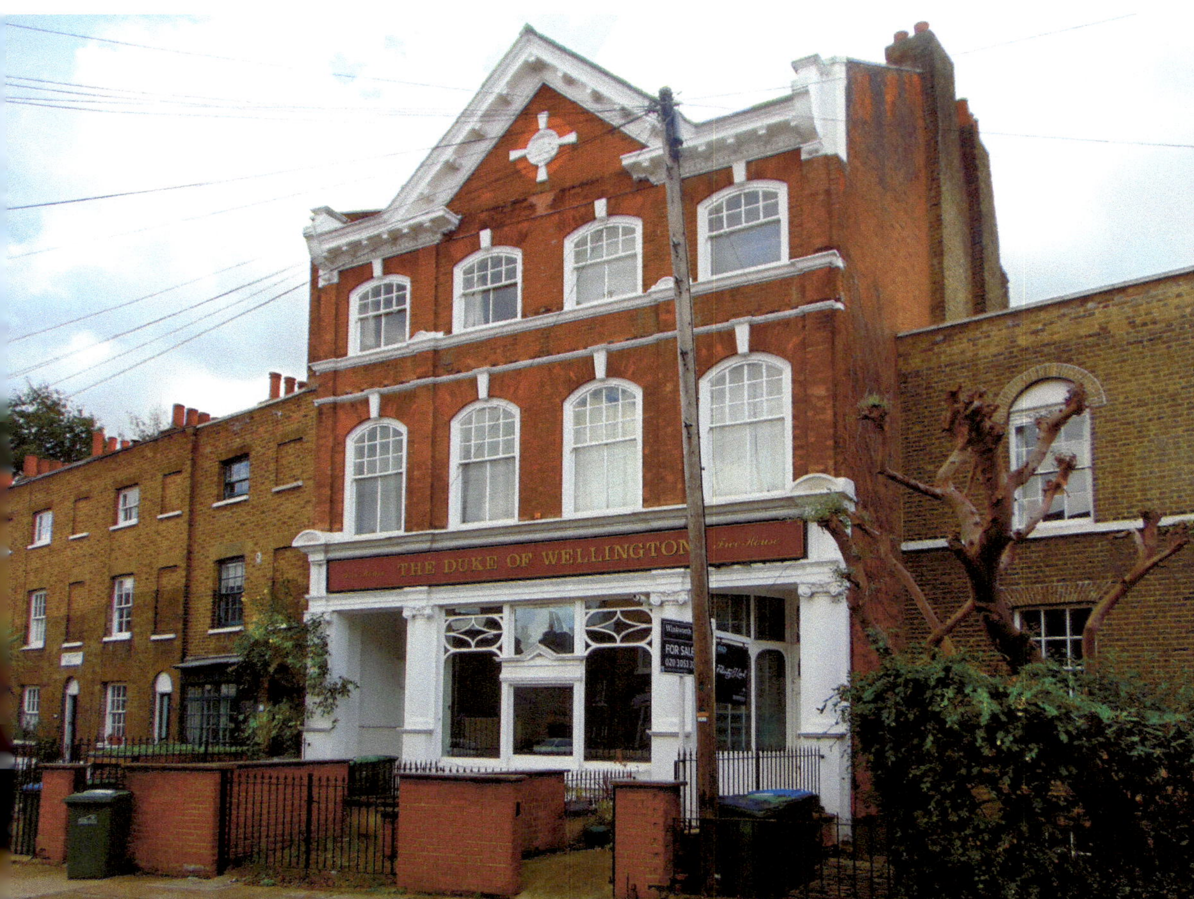

The pubs that have survived across East Greenwich, along with recently opened bars and microbreweries, are now mostly frequented by a community of new residents moving into the area, along with a few tourists venturing out from the town centre, students attending the University of Greenwich, and a number of longstanding locals who continue to reside in the eastern side of Greenwich.

THE PLUME OF FEATHERS, Park Vista

Reputed to be the oldest surviving public house in Greenwich, the Plume of Feathers is also the closest pub to the Meridian Line, situated just within the globe's Eastern Hemisphere.

Erected in 1691, on freehold land of the Lordship of East Greenwich, the inn was first known as the Prince of Wales, located on the original main thoroughfare from the town centre, where stagecoach passengers, travellers and cattle drovers passing through the Queens House Gate would stop for refreshment before heading out into deepest Kent.

On a 1695 map, attributed to Surveyor General Samuel Travers, the area is shown as consisting of large areas of open land around the time the pub was erected.

The pub appears in the 1717 parish rate books, recording that John Issacs, possibly the landlord, paid ten shillings and ninepence on the property. After landlady Jane Whitall took over the public house in 1726, the name changed to the Plume of

The Plume of Feathers, closest pub east of the Meridian Line.

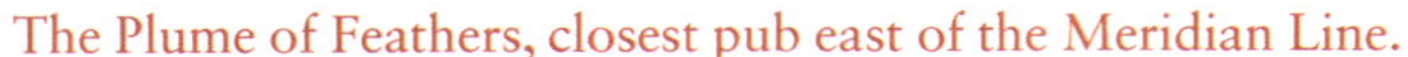

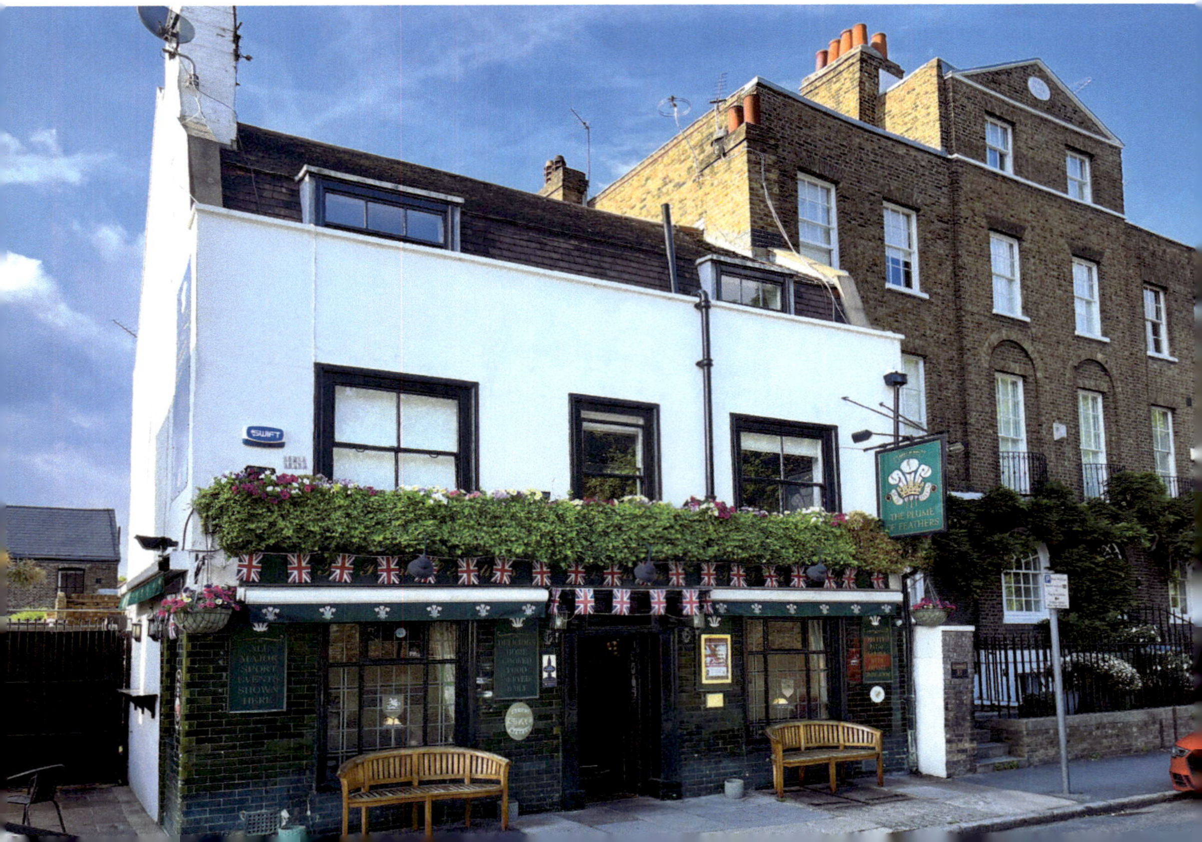

Feathers, the heraldic emblem of the Prince of Wales, traced back to Edward, the Black Prince, whose eldest sister, Princess Isabella Plantagenet, was buried at Greyfriars Church, Greenwich. Around the late eighteenth century, it is believed that the pub and an adjacent cottage, owned by the landlord, were then knocked into one property.

With the increase of traffic heading into Kent, a wider highway, Romney Road, named after park ranger Lord Romney, was built during the late seventeenth century further north from Park Place, which then left the Plume of Feathers sidelined away from this main new thoroughfare, and the pub took on the identity of a typical example of a country village local.

Although the structure of the Plume of Feathers has altered slightly over the years, the charm and atmosphere of a village pub still exists today. The Plume of Feathers had been a tied public house under several breweries, including Watney's, Truman's, Courage and Scottish and Newcastle.

After Jimmy Rose and his wife Sue acquired the licence in 1980, towards the mid-1990s, they made a few further alterations to the pub by extending the kitchen and adding a seated dining area to the rear.

Independent landlords since 1999, Sue and son James became tie free, and now stock a variety of beers, the Plume of Feathers holding Cask Marque Awards for serving quality real ale. The pub by Greenwich Park is renowned for its home-cooked fayre, especially its Sunday roasts.

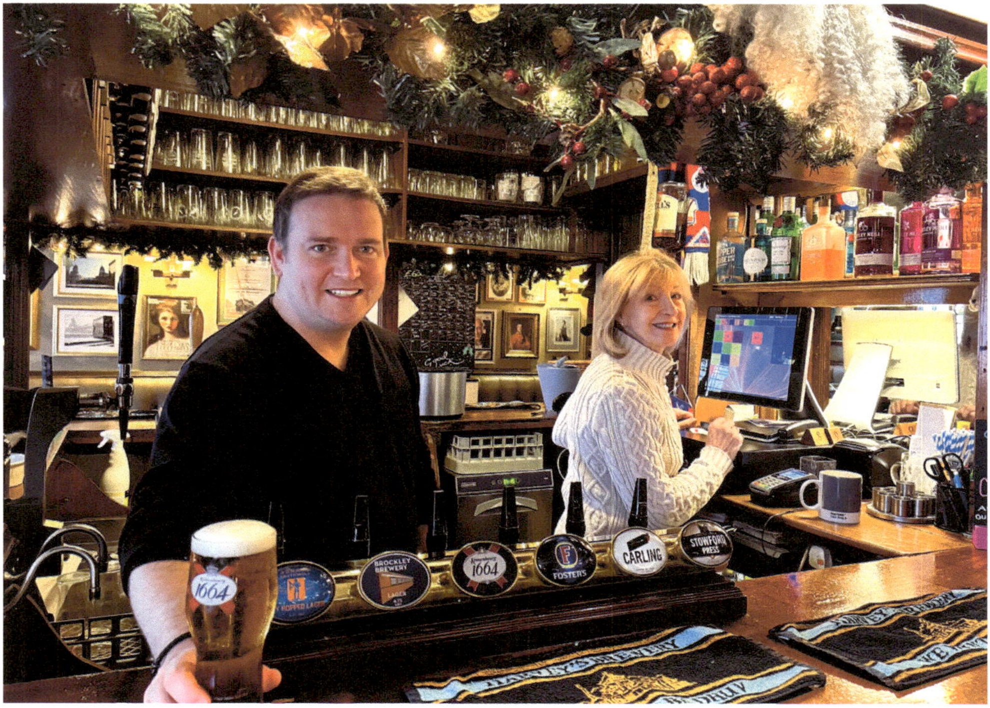

The Plume of Feathers proprietors James and Sue Rose.

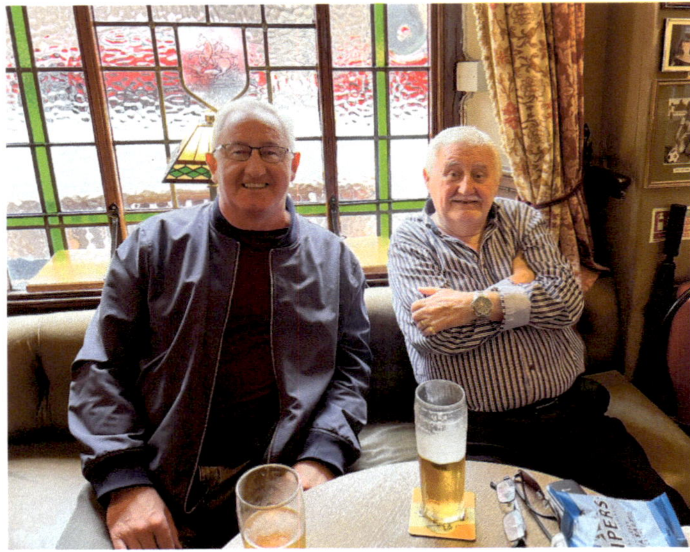

Two of the Plume
of Feathers regulars,
Brian Little and David
Goggin, with plenty
of stories about their
local pubs to tell.

THE STAR OF GREENWICH, Old Woolwich Road

One of the last surviving pubs on the street where I once lived, the Star & Garter, as it was once known, came near to closing for good in the summer of 2021, when an altercation between two regulars resulted in a stabbing and loss of the landlord's licence.

Believed to have been erected on the site of a previous pub, the White Bear, dating to the late 1600s, the Star & Garter was built during the early nineteenth century,

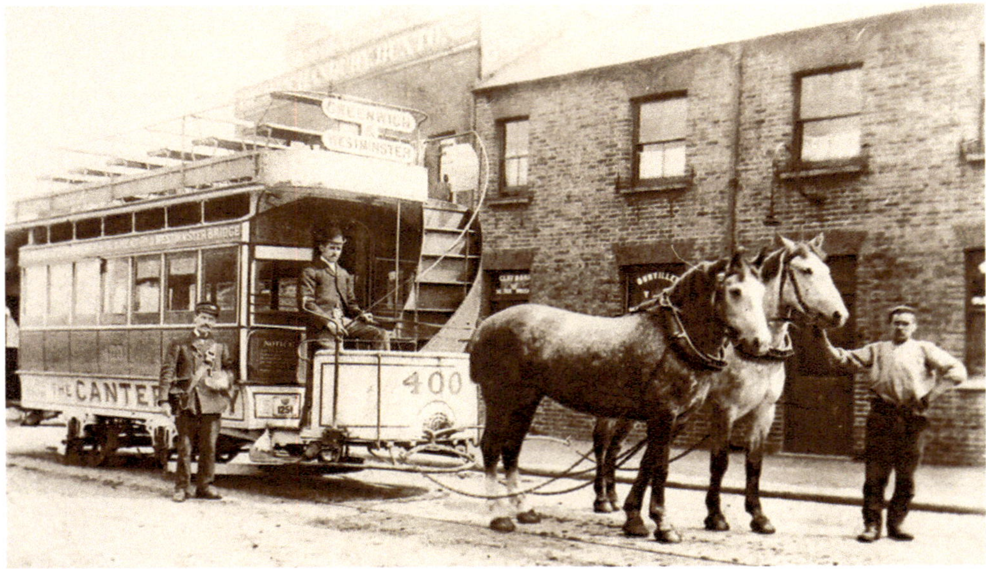

Horse-drawn tram outside the Star & Garter, late 1800s.

adjacent to a tram depot. The busy large backstreet boozer was mostly used by local workers, many employed at Greenwich Power Station, built on the tram site opposite and completed in 1910.

The Star, as we called the pub, became one of my first regular drinking places where I would meet up with friends to play darts matches or when getting together for a few beers on a Saturday before making our way to watch Charlton Athletic playing at The Valley, just under 2 miles to the east. The first landlord of the Star who I remember was Mick Grady, a humorous Irishman who loved a drink, often turning the phrase 'what do you think this is, a Speak Easy?'. Although always keeping the house in order, it was not unusual for drinking to carry on long after Mick had called time. When Mick and his wife moved on, their successors carried on the tradition of serving a few rounds of drinks well after closing.

It was at the Star where I was also casually employed, once a week on a Friday evening, while still attending secondary school, playing a selection of the latest hits and golden oldies for the pub's regulars. Aided by my friend Geoff, playing vinyl discs on a state-of-the-art twin deck record mixer, we were paid the sum of five bob each (five shillings, equivalent to fifty pence), the music night an attempt to bring in a few more customers when pub discos were becoming popular.

The Star of Greenwich after reopening in 2023.

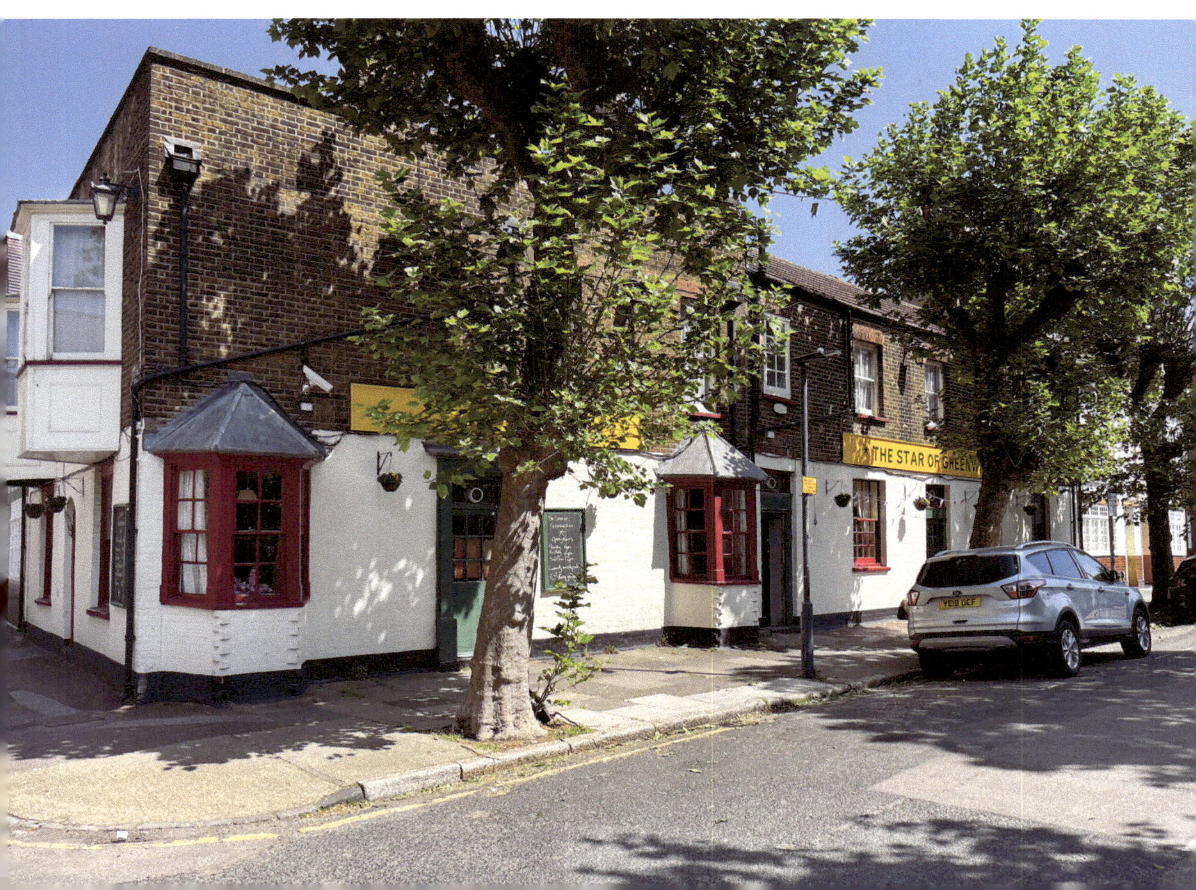

After the Star & Garter lost its trading licence in 2022, the property's owner, Greenwich Hospital Charity, a major landowner in Greenwich, then decided to put the pub up for sale. However, listed as an Asset of Community Value, any local community groups interested in taking the pub over had the opportunity to put in an offer first.

A group of locals, and Star & Garter devotees, came together in a bid to relaunch the Star as a radically inclusive community pub, creating a space for groups to meet, and hosting a range of community activities and educational workshops, as well as continuing to serve drinks. In November 2022, after a council licensing committee meeting, it was announced the pub would be granted a new licence under a new name: the Star of Greenwich. Planning to launch a community share offer to fund the three-year lease with the freeholders, Greenwich Hospital Charity, the pub, under the new name the Star of Greenwich, reopened to the public and wider community after some refurbishment and redecoration both inside and out.

HARDY'S, Trafalgar Road

Dating from the mid to late 1800s, when the pub was built, situated centrally in a row of properties on the main thoroughfare through Greenwich, it was named the Bricklayers Arms, a period when many shops, houses and industrial buildings were being constructed eastwards from Greenwich Hospital.

Hardy's, one of two surviving pubs on Trafalgar Road.

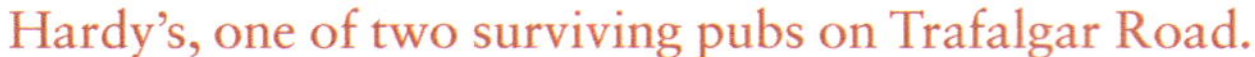

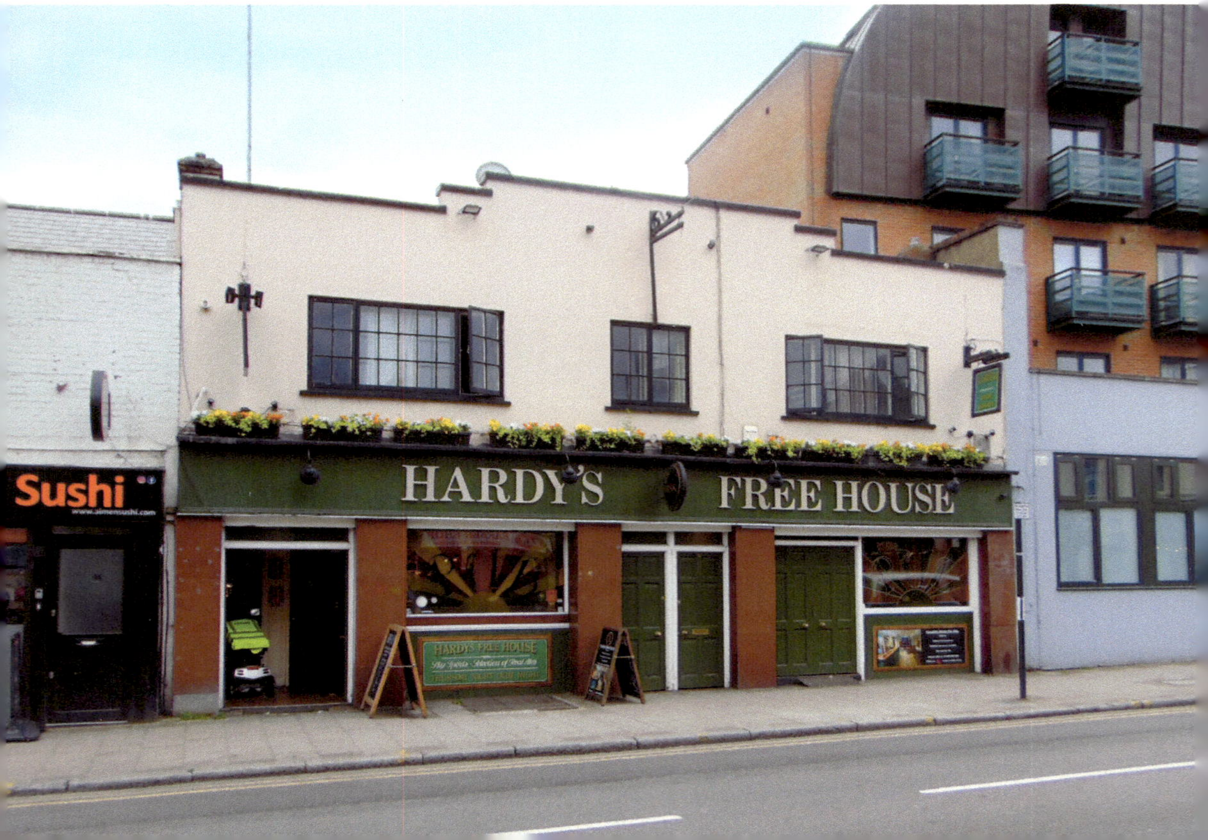

At the time the pub was built, as a way of bringing in custom, public houses often took the name of a trade, as workers would often search out pubs associated with their profession. With many bricklayers arriving to seek out employment in Greenwich, it is likely this is why the Bricklayers Arms acquired its name. The pub opened a few years before East Greenwich Power Station was erected, a huge structure with four tall chimneys built of London Stock brick, the development employing hundreds of bricklayers and the pub benefitting from their custom during the eight years it took to build the power station.

In the early 1920s, the Bricklayers Arms expanded its premises into an adjoining shop, situated between the pub and picture theatre, and leading up towards the Second World War, the pub went through a substantial refurbishment, where the Victorian frontage was replaced by a simple plain art deco-style plastered upper façade, with rectangular steel-framed picture windows and supporting tiled pillars below, the ground-floor windows and doors also consisting of a much more modernist design.

The Bricklayers Arms was the very first pub I would go to with friends, a couple of times a week back in the early 1970s, where we would meet up during the evening, all of us slightly below the legal drinking age, spending my two shillings and sixpence on a bottle of Mackeson Milk Stout and a packet of crisps and playing games of snooker.

A onetime Charrington's tied pub, in the latter part of the 1900s, the Bricklayers Arms was renamed Hardy's, after Vice Admiral Sir Thomas Hardy, who served as flag captain to Admiral Lord Nelson on HMS *Victory*.

After various internal refurbishments during the following years, Hardy's became an Irish-themed freehouse, with one long bar and several large screens for showing live sport events, and an area for dining in the former adjoining shop.

In 2004, Hardy's was voted tenth most popular London boozer in a poll carried out by Beer in the Evening pub and bar guide.

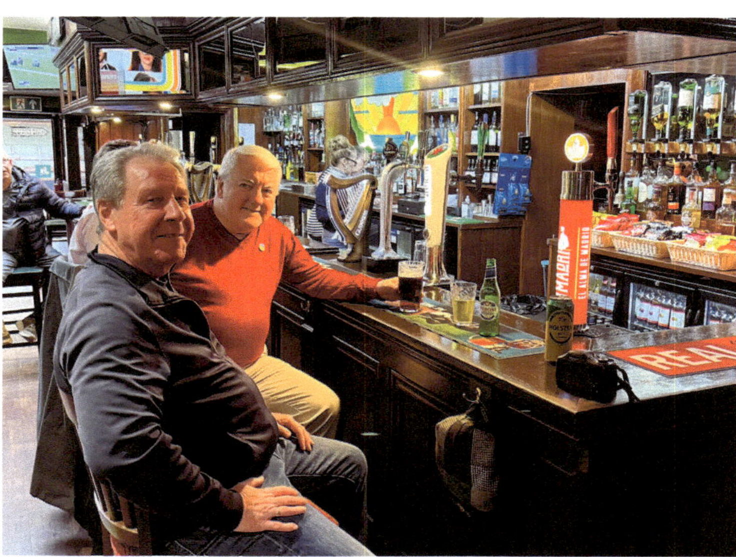

Two local drinkers and Greenwich residents Les Henry and Geoff Billingsley, in Hardy's.

THE PELTON ARMS, Pelton Road

Over the years many Greenwich pubs have had a change of name; however, there is one which displays two names, the Pelton Arms and the Nags Head.

When north-east coal merchant William Cole Child negotiated the lease of Morden College owned land on Greenwich Marsh, to establish a riverside wharf and works to expand his coal, cement, and iron trading business into the south, Cole Child was required to make improvements to land drainage and road access, as well as providing finance to develop residential properties erected on Pelton Road, which included a public house built at the end of the row.

After completion of the industrial works around 1840, the pub was the next to be erected, named the Pelton Arms after Pelton Colliery, County Durham.

The Pelton, as most locals referred to the pub, stayed much the same throughout the years as when first built, situated on the corner block of houses, the pub's bars consisting of a saloon, public and snug, along with a shop for off-sales. The interior Victorian style décor also remained in a similar fashion up until the late 1900s.

When Hollywood came to Greenwich in 1963, the Pelton was another local pub used as a backdrop in the film *The List of Adrian Messenger*.

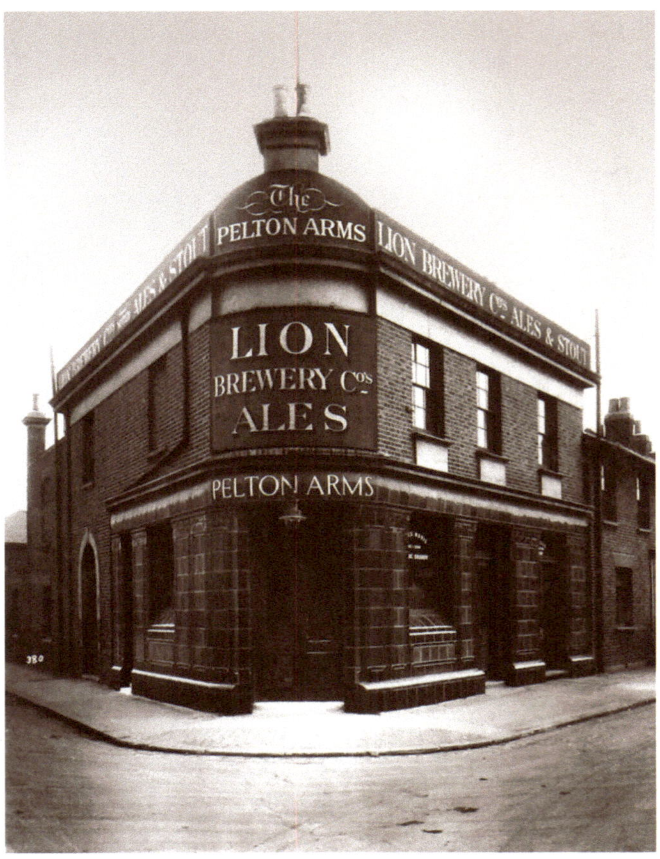

The Pelton Arms, early 1900s.

After coming under the management of landlord Geoff Keen, before refurbished, the pub was once again used as a filming location for the television production *Rock and Chips*, set in the 1960s, a prequel to the popular comedy series *Only Fools and Horses*, the Pelton Arms doubling as the Nags Head, Del Boy and Rodney's local boozer. After

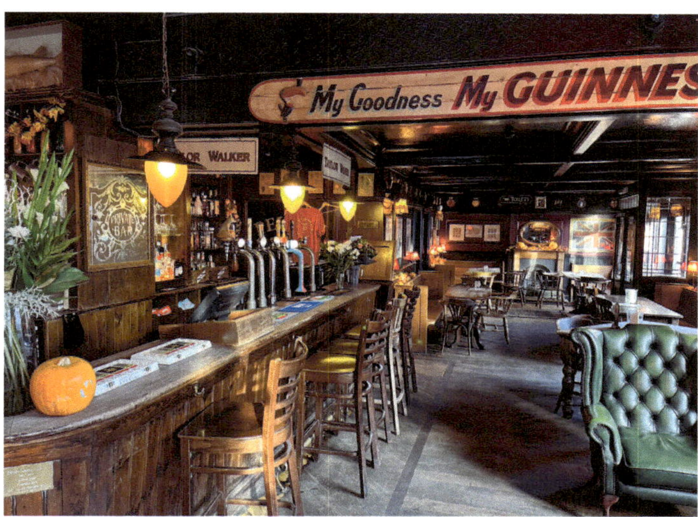

Above: Refurbished bar of the Pelton Arms after filming *Rock and Chips*.

Below: The Pelton Arms, a colliery pub in Greenwich.

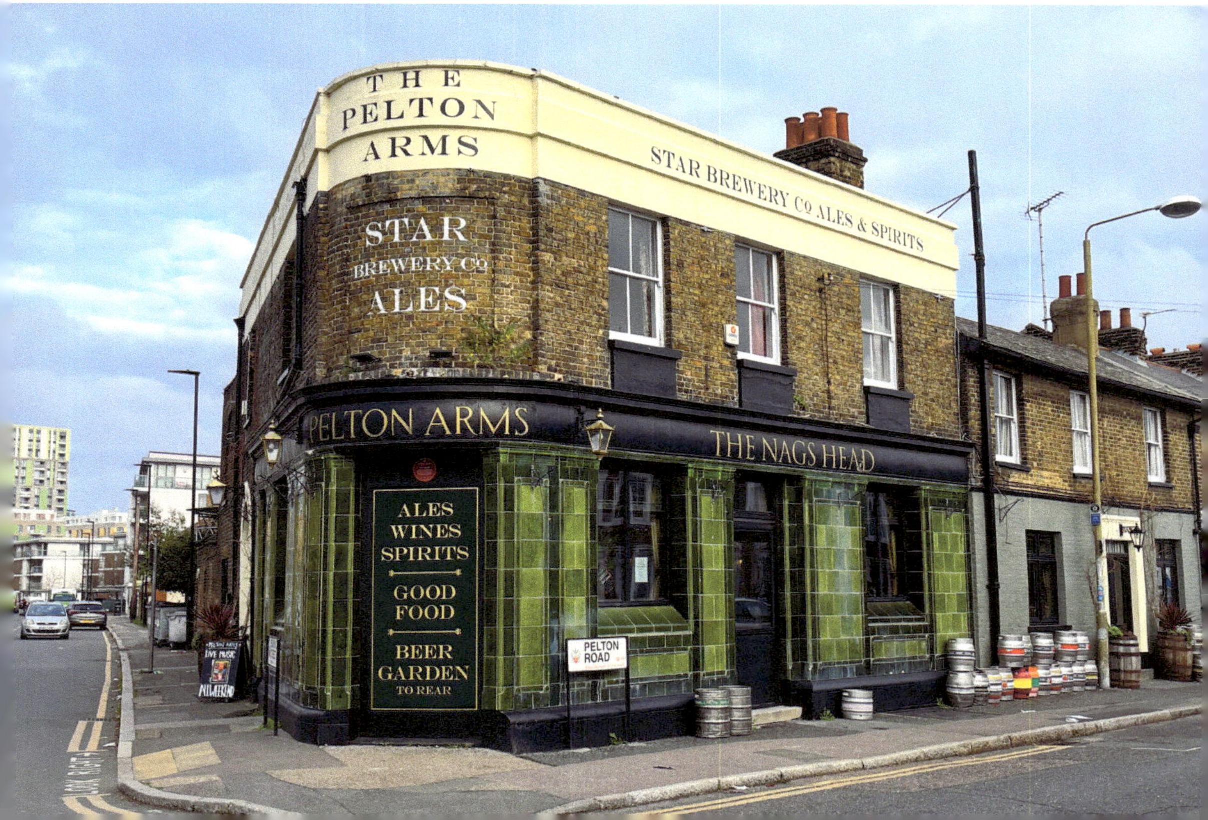

filming was completed, the Nags Head signage was left in place on the outer south facing side of the pub.

With a new modish-styled interior, the Pelton, serving a variety of beers, real ales, and food, holds various events for the local community, including quizzes and live music nights, where members of Squeeze have performed. Two of the group, Chris Difford and Glen Tilbrook, are both local Greenwich lads.

THE CROWN, Trafalgar Road

Situated at a corner plot facing onto the main Greenwich thoroughfare, the Crown was built during the early 1840s, on the edge of former orchards, a time when much of East Greenwich was mostly farmland and meadows.

A majority of pubs during the nineteenth century began selling just beer, the licensing laws requiring a landlord to obtain another licence to sell spirits, and when the Crown's first landlord Richard Wheatley applied for a spirit licence in September 1946, he was refused.

There were various reasons justices rejected an application for a spirit licence. In many cases it was because the applicant could not satisfy the justices they were not just selling beer simply to obtain a spirit licence, the selling of spirits being more

The Crown, the closest pub to the former home of the author.

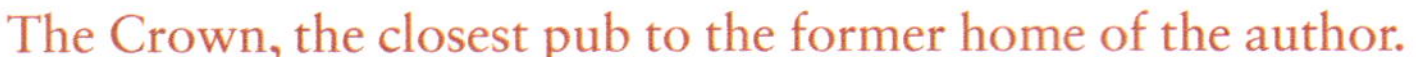

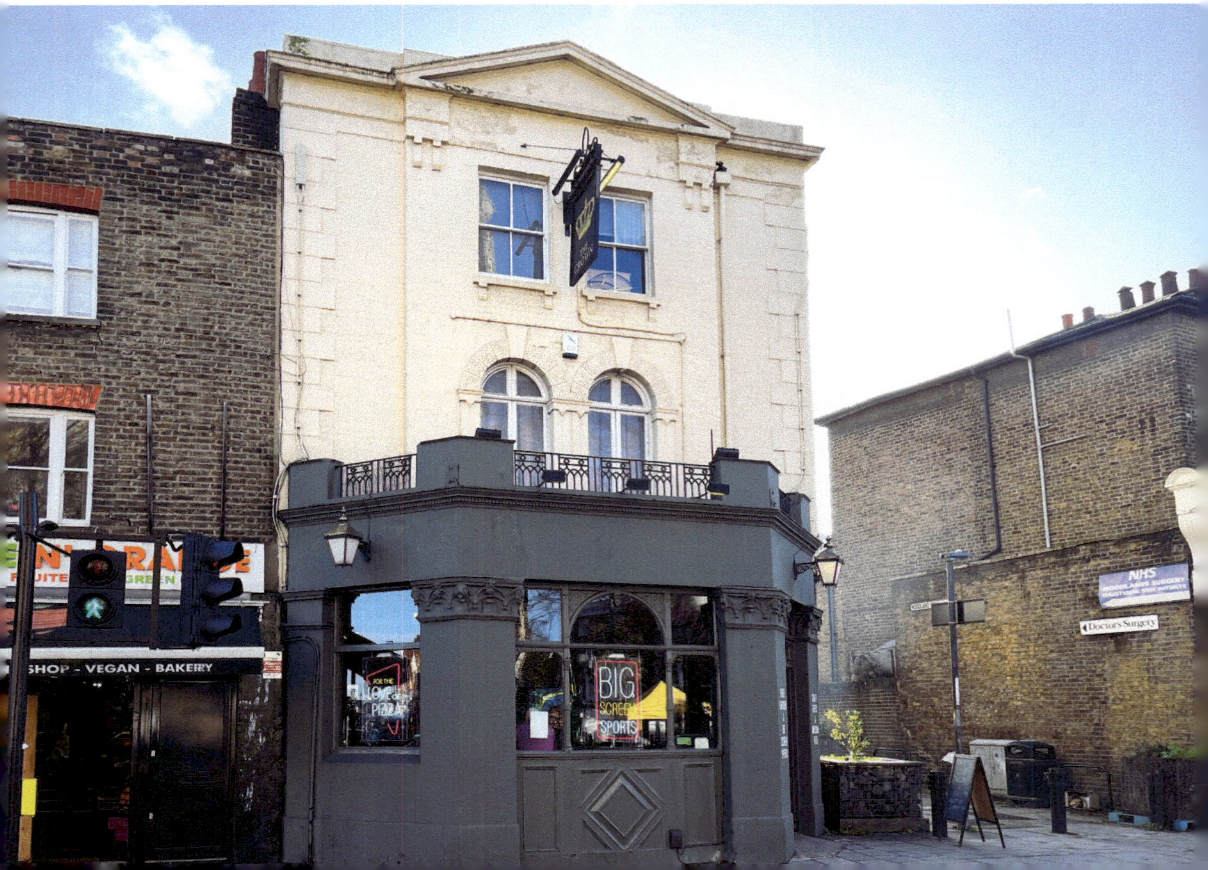

lucrative, and at a time when there had been a dependency by the poorer classes on the consumption of gin.

The Crown emerged from the nineteenth century to become a flourishing old-time community boozer, with a public bar at the front and a saloon bar to the rear, accessed via a narrow lane to the side of the pub. The interior featured a long carved dark wood bar, backed by high panelled etched glass mirrors, which have survived several refurbishments.

The Crown, the closet pub to our family home on Old Woolwich Road, was my father's and his friends' local when the licensee, known as Irish John, along with his wife Molly, ran the pub. On Sunday afternoons, before the official closing time of 3.00 p.m., although drinking-up time would go on until much later, a variety of south-east London-style tapas would be placed out on the bar – dishes of shrimps, cockles, winkles, whelks and prawns, accompanied by cheese and biscuits, roast potatoes, and slices of Yorkshire pudding, a few appetizers – before going home for a late Sunday roast.

After the popular landlord retired and returned to Ireland, the Crown went through a succession of licensees and managers, and then went through a modern refurbishment when acquired by Frontier Pubs, a joint venture between Enterprise Inns and London gastropub operation Food & Fuel, the company designing their pubs as local community hubs, focusing on craft beers and homemade pizzas.

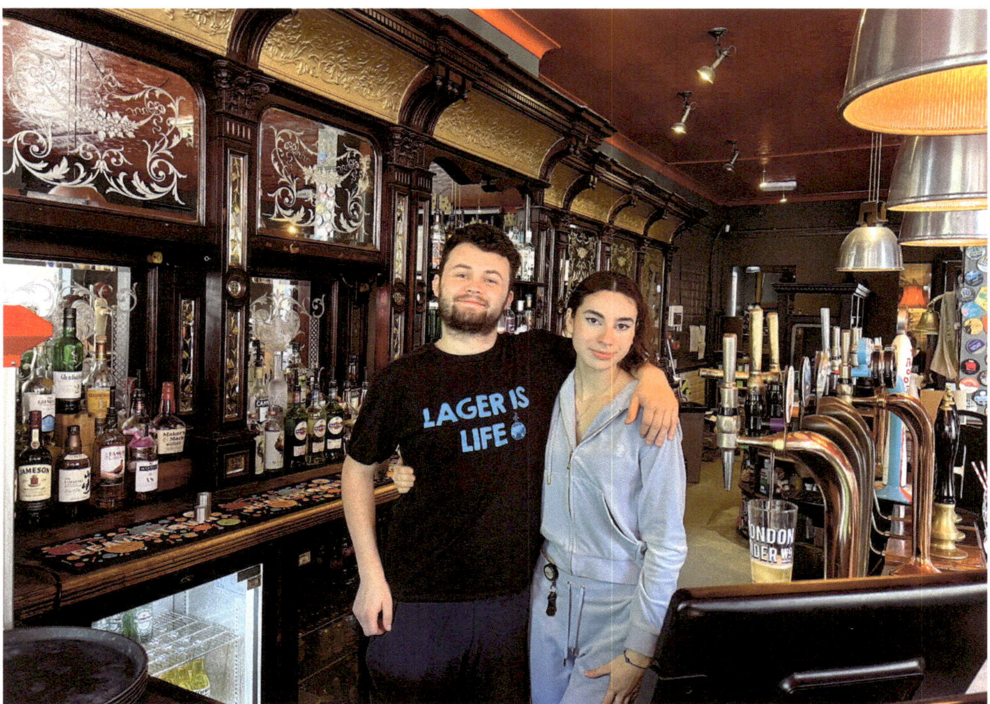

General manager of the Crown Paddy and assistant Giselle.

THE VANBRUGH TAVERN, Colomb Street

Located on one of East Greenwich's backstreets, the Vanbrugh Tavern, erected on a corner of a row of terraced houses in the late 1800s, was originally named the Duke of Edinburgh when Colomb Street was also known by another name – George Street South.

At the time the pub was built, the title Duke of Edinburgh was held by Queen Victoria's second son, Alfred, up until his death in 1900, the title then recreated by King George VI, bestowed on his son-in-law Phillip Mountbatten, the prince also holding the subsidiary title Baron of Greenwich.

Typical of a pub from the period, locals had the choice of two bars to drink in, a saloon and a public bar. The Duke of Edinburgh also had a small area to the front of the pub for off-sales. The licencing laws at the time only permitted beer to be drunk on the premises unless the pub held an off-sales licence, which allowed beer sold over the counter to be taken away to drink at home.

It was customary in the mid-1900s for children to earn some pocket money by taking empty beer bottles back to the off-sales, collecting the money from the deposit on the bottles, a job my friends and I used to do too, buying packets of crisps or a large arrowroot biscuit, kept in a big glass jar on the bar counter, with the bottle deposit returns.

Sun setting on the Vanbrugh Tavern.

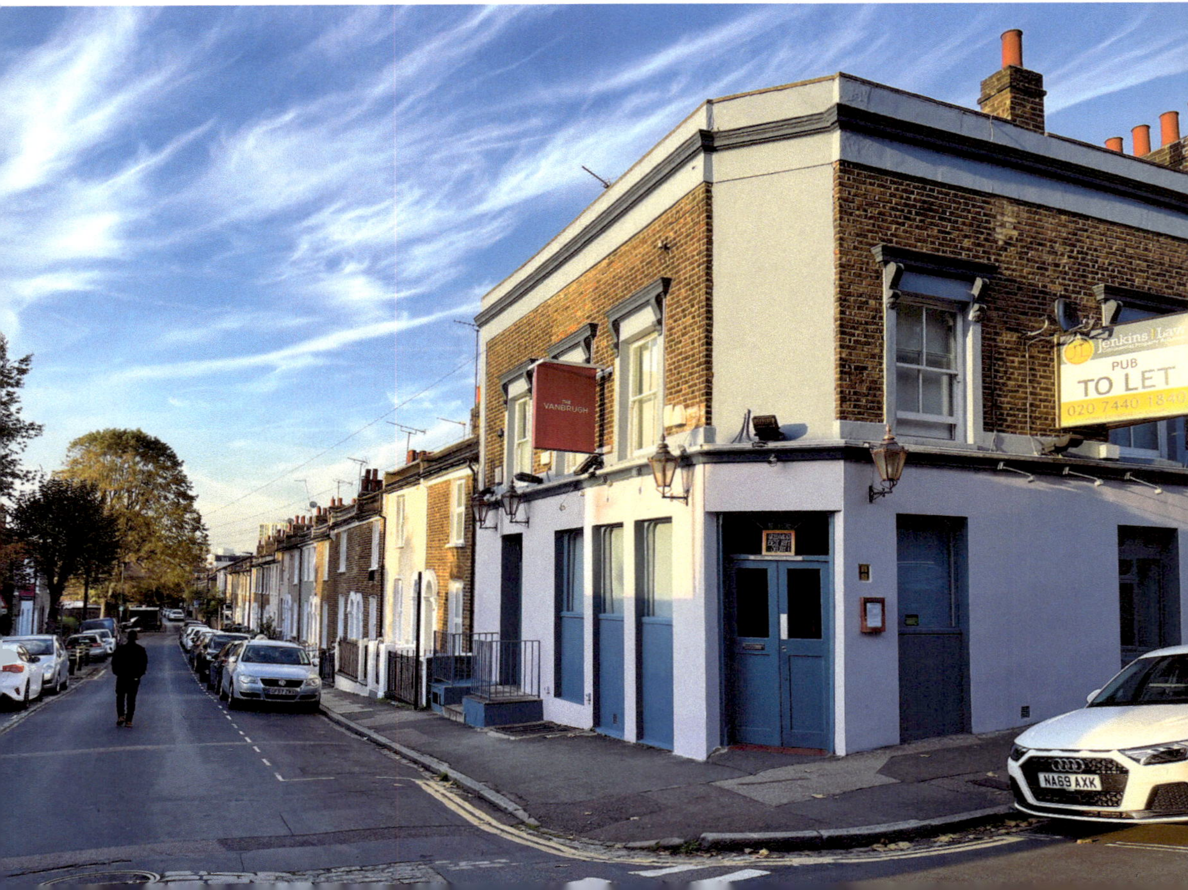

Surviving through the war years, after a succession of licensees, the Duke of Edinburgh's name changed to the Vanbrugh Tavern during the late 1900s. The name Vanbrugh was chosen as the pub was in close proximity to Vanbrugh Hill and Vanbrugh Castle at the top of Maze Hill, both named after Sir John Vanbrugh, dramatist, architect and suspected spy for the British Government. Vanbrugh, a resident of Greenwich, lived with his family in the castle he designed and commissioned to be built in the early 1700s, while serving as Surveyor to the Royal Hospital.

In the summer of 2022, after eighteen years at the Vanbrugh Tavern, popular landlady JoJo finally called time on her tenancy, the pub closing temporarily until a new landlord or landlady takes over.

THE THAI TIGER, Woolwich Road

When Blackwall Lane was nothing more than a track, known as Marsh Lane, running north onto Greenwich Level, also later known as Greenwich Marsh, a large coaching inn was erected to the southern end of the lane during the late eighteenth century, named the Ship & Billet. The inn became a popular place for Greenwich residents to travel to from the town's centre, by horse, or horse and carriage, where they would socialise by having a few glasses of fine wine or ale while dining, and partake in various games played in the pub's large garden.

As Greenwich Level evolved into an area of industry during the mid-1800s, the inn was rebuilt and from then onwards would be mainly frequented by workers employed in the local industries, rather than a higher class of clientele who once journeyed out from West Greenwich and Blackheath, the pub hosting various community events for

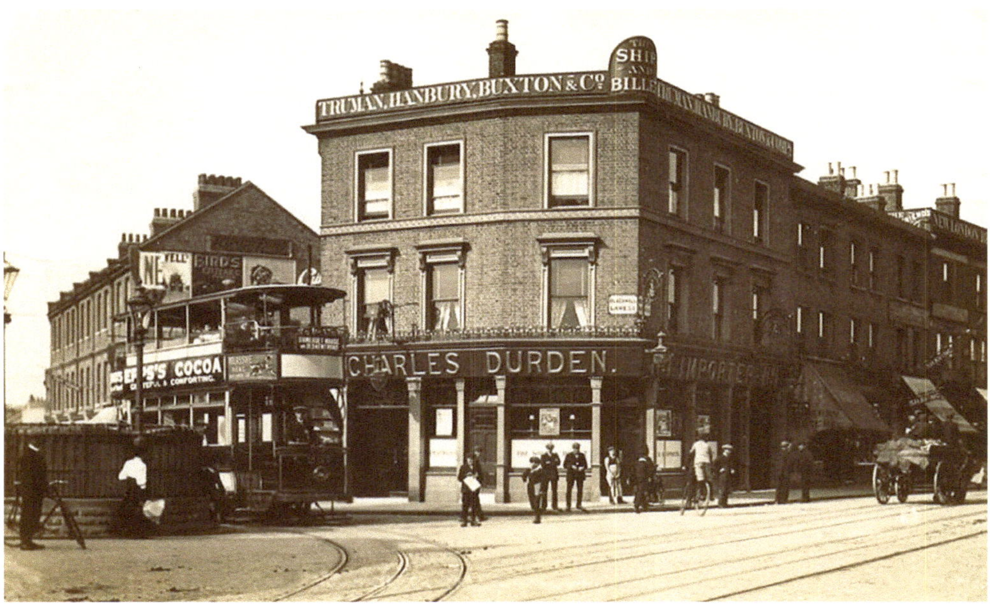

The Ship & Billet, after it was rebuilt in the mid-1800s.

the local workers, and local residents and their families, which included pedestrian racing, a popular sport where spectators placed bets on these competitive foot races.

Under a succession of licensees, the Ship & Billet, taken over by Yates Taverns in 1944, continued to be a popular drinking place for locals living and employed at East Greenwich industries. However, leading up towards the end of the twentieth century, the pub, leased by Truman's Brewery, had fallen on hard times. After a makeover in the 1980s, the landlady renamed the pub The Frog and Radiator, as she wanted a distinctive and amusing new title.

At the beginning of the twenty-first century the pub's name reverted to the Ship & Billet, before changing again, this time to the Duchess, and then, prior to its closure in 2017, to the Duchess of Greenwich. The pub's closure was forced when the licence was withdrawn after council licencing officers, carrying out an inspection, discovered the pub was being run by a group of obnoxious regulars, operating unregular hours, the landlord nowhere to be found.

The old pub stood vacant after closure until reopening in 2018 as a bar and restaurant, Thai Tiger, specialising, as the name suggests, in a range of authentic Thai dishes, and like many modern-day public houses, relying on serving food as well as drinks as a means to survive.

Thai Tiger, formerly the Duchess of Greenwich.

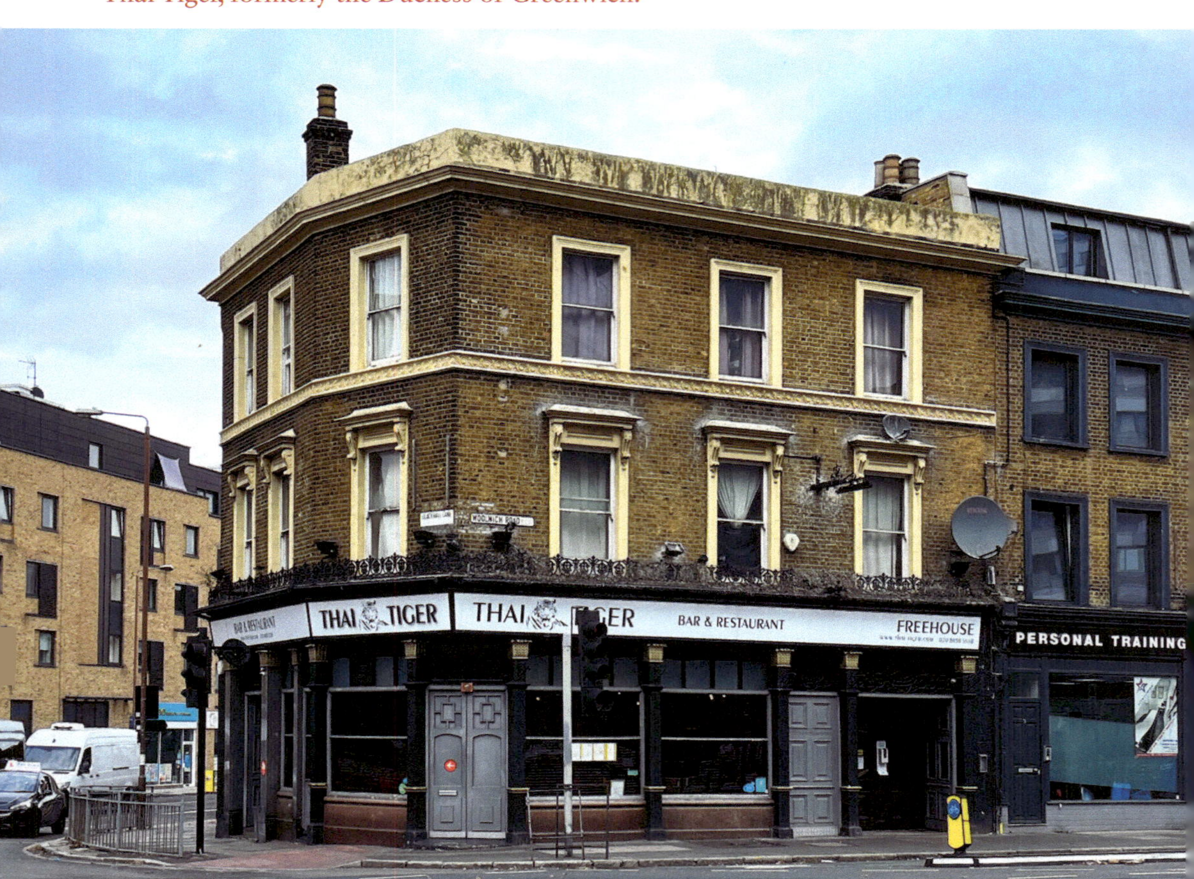

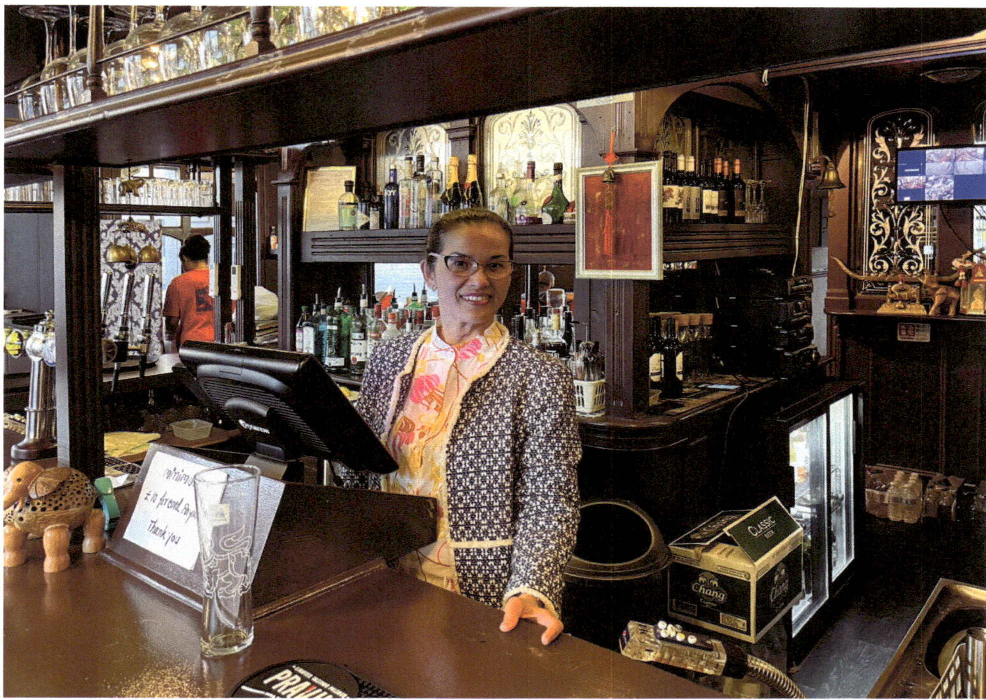

Manager of the Thai Tiger Soothira Gray.

MEANTIME, Blackwall Lane

Since the time when Greenwich Marsh first became an area of shipbuilding and industry, various pubs and beerhouses had once existed on this large expanse of land, built to serve a growing community of workers and their families. The first of the new modern beer drinking establishments erected on Greenwich Marsh, renamed Greenwich Peninsula, is Meantime Brewery, a pioneer in brewing craft ale and lager.

Founded in 1999 by university post-graduate in brewing and bio-chemistry Alastair Hook, who began brewing historic beers in a small Charlton industrial lock-up, Meantime moved into the new £1.9 million state-of-the-art brewery on Blackwall Lane in 2010, and by 2017 had expanded its premises to include a shop, tasting rooms and bar serving a selection of craft beers, such as a traditional London Pale Ale, and a new brewery designed beer, Chocolate Porter, the original porter a popular brew of the porters working at London markets. The bar area also serves a variety of food dishes, as well as holding pie and pint nights, reminiscent of the days when many Greenwich pubs sold hot pies from over the counter along with a pint.

At the Moeschle brewing facility, Moeschle referring to the large stainless-steel brewing tanks, originally used in making wine, Meantime runs group brewery tours and tutored tastings, where visitors can sample a variety of the brewery's historic beers.

Increasing beer, ale, and lager production to over 120 hectolitres a year, equivalent to 2.6 million gallons, the bar is unlikely to ever run dry on the busiest of nights.

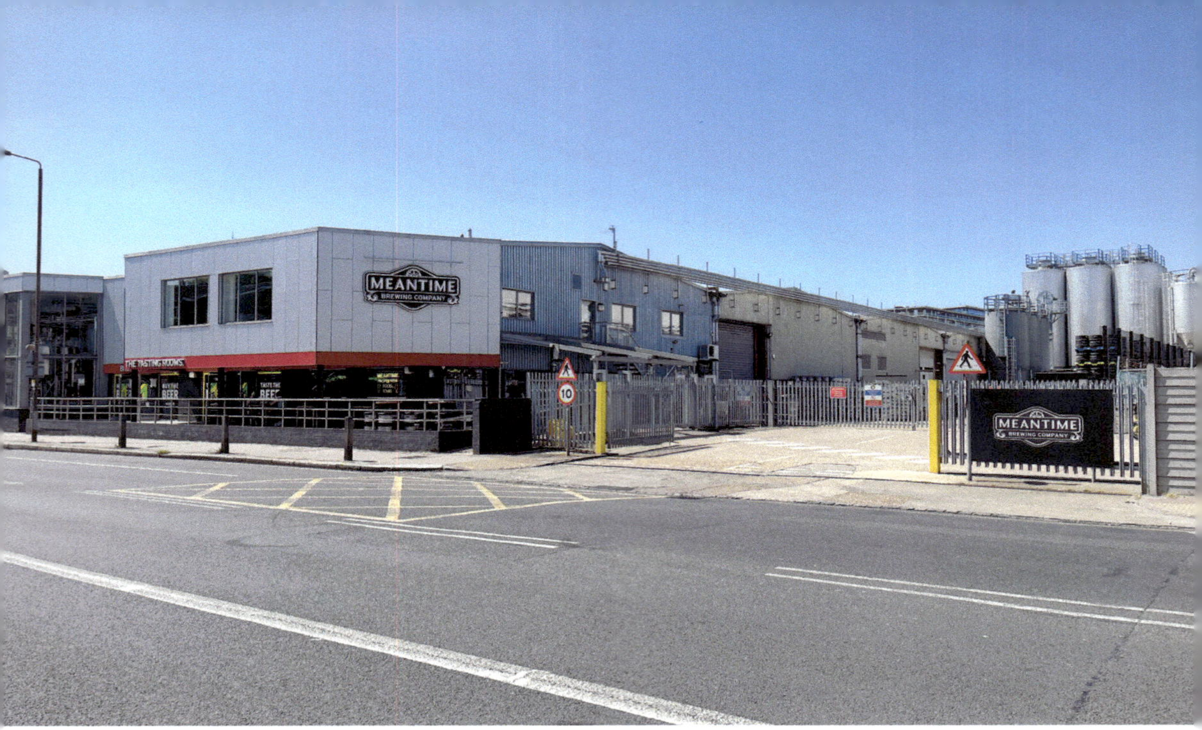

Above: Meantime brewery on Greenwich Marsh.

Below: Meantime general manager Buddy on duty in the summer, 2022.

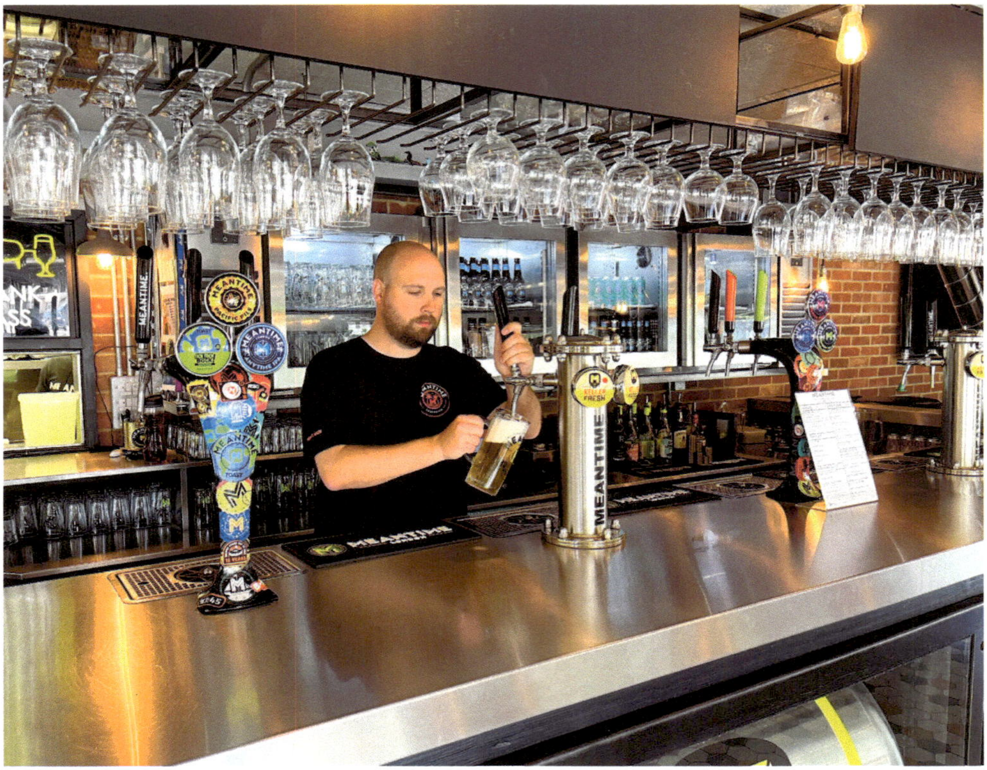

Winning many brewing awards, Meantime was purchased in 2015 by the world's second largest brewer, SAB Miller, and just under a year after Meantime was acquired by Asahi Group Holdings.

As well as serving its own brewed craft beer at its Blackwall Lane facility, Meantime also distributes its brews nationally and internationally, and has become a well-regarded hub of the local community, holding fun theme nights and festivals, with plenty of beer on tap and in bottles and cans.

THE RIVER ALE HOUSE, Woolwich Road

Opened in September 2017, the River Ale House occupies a former lingerie corner shop originally named Under Cover Experience, owned by Trevor Puddifoot, who decided to switch from selling underwear to selling beer, a new venture in partnership with his daughter Sian and son Joe.

After conversion and refurbishment, the lingerie shop became a micropub, serving a range of dark and light gravity cask ales, Belgian beers, ciders and wines, alongside various spirits, all served from the front of shop counter. Split over two levels, the bar at the front and a drinking area on a slightly lower level to the rear, the rooms are

The River Ale House, the first micropub to open in Greenwich.

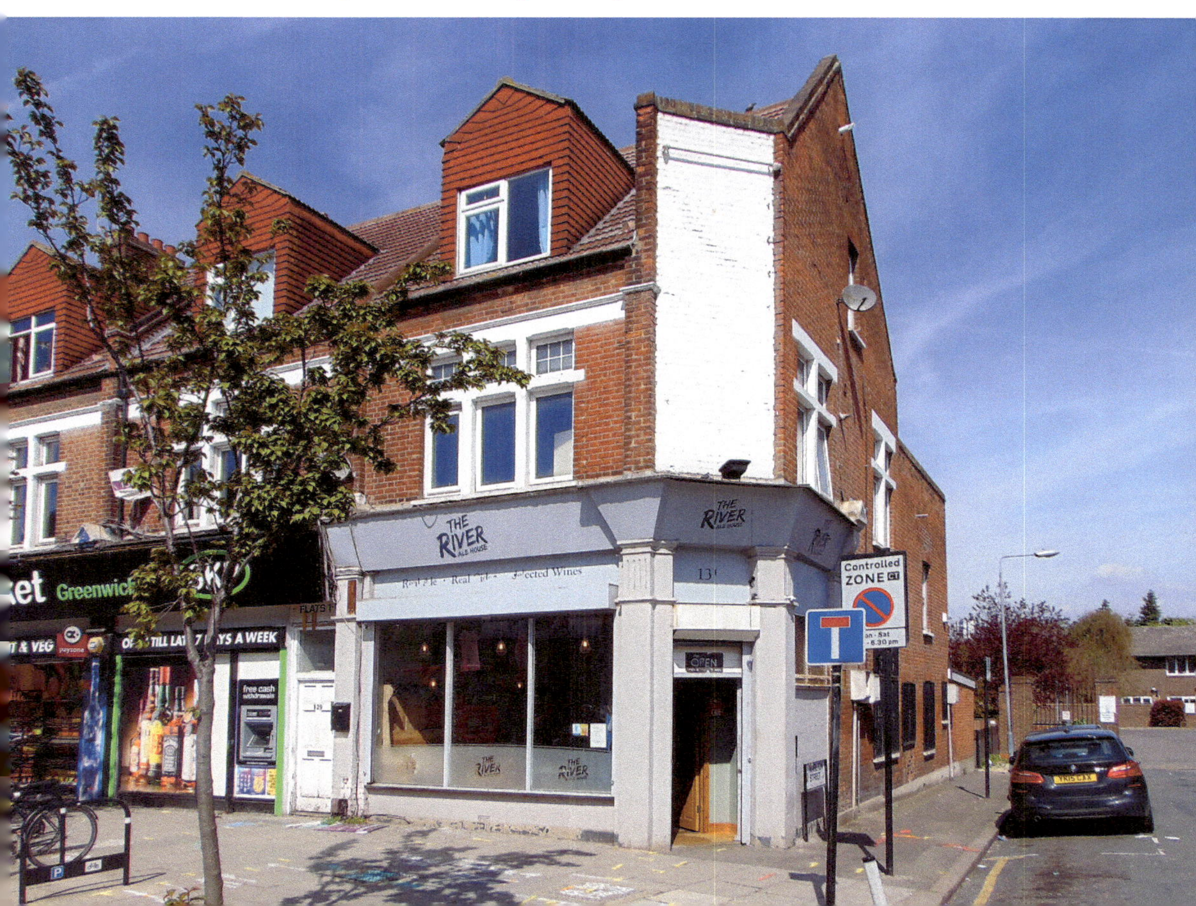

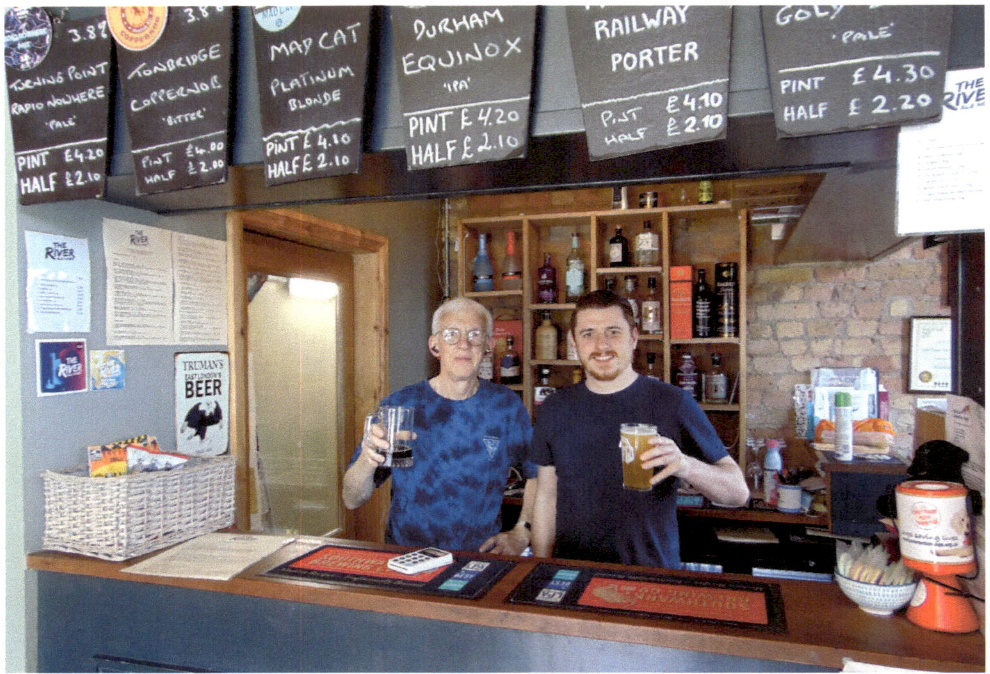

Proprietors of the River Ale House Trevor Puddifoot and son Joe.

simply decorated with exposed brick walls, wood panelling and wooden floors, the tables and seating made from reclaimed wood and scaffold boards, complemented by high tables and settles, where patrons can sit and relax with a pint.

The soft illuminations from hanging pendant lamps and wall lights give the micropub a warm welcoming glow to attract customers inside, the passers-by venturing inside joined by beer drinkers arriving from all parts of Greenwich to sample real ale at the riverside town's first micropub, evocative of the beerhouses of long ago.

Proprietor Trevor is a huge Bruce Springsteen fan, and you will often hear tunes from the 'Boss' playing in the background while the regulars are enjoying a beer or cider in the micropub's bars. Voted pub of the year in south-east London by members of CAMRA in 2022, the River Ale House also won Cider Pub of the Year for the second year running.

THE ANGERSTEIN HOTEL, Woolwich Road

The imposing Angerstein Hotel, built in 1888 on the corner plot of Woolwich Road and Combedale Road, was named after John Julius Angerstein, a local industrialist, Lloyds underwriter and dignitary who owned land in East Greenwich and a large property and estate, the Woodlands, once part of the old Manor of Westcombe, laying to the south of the hotel.

Erected over three storeys with attic rooms, as with a majority of large Victorian pubs, the high-ceilinged ground floor was divided into public and saloon bars, the

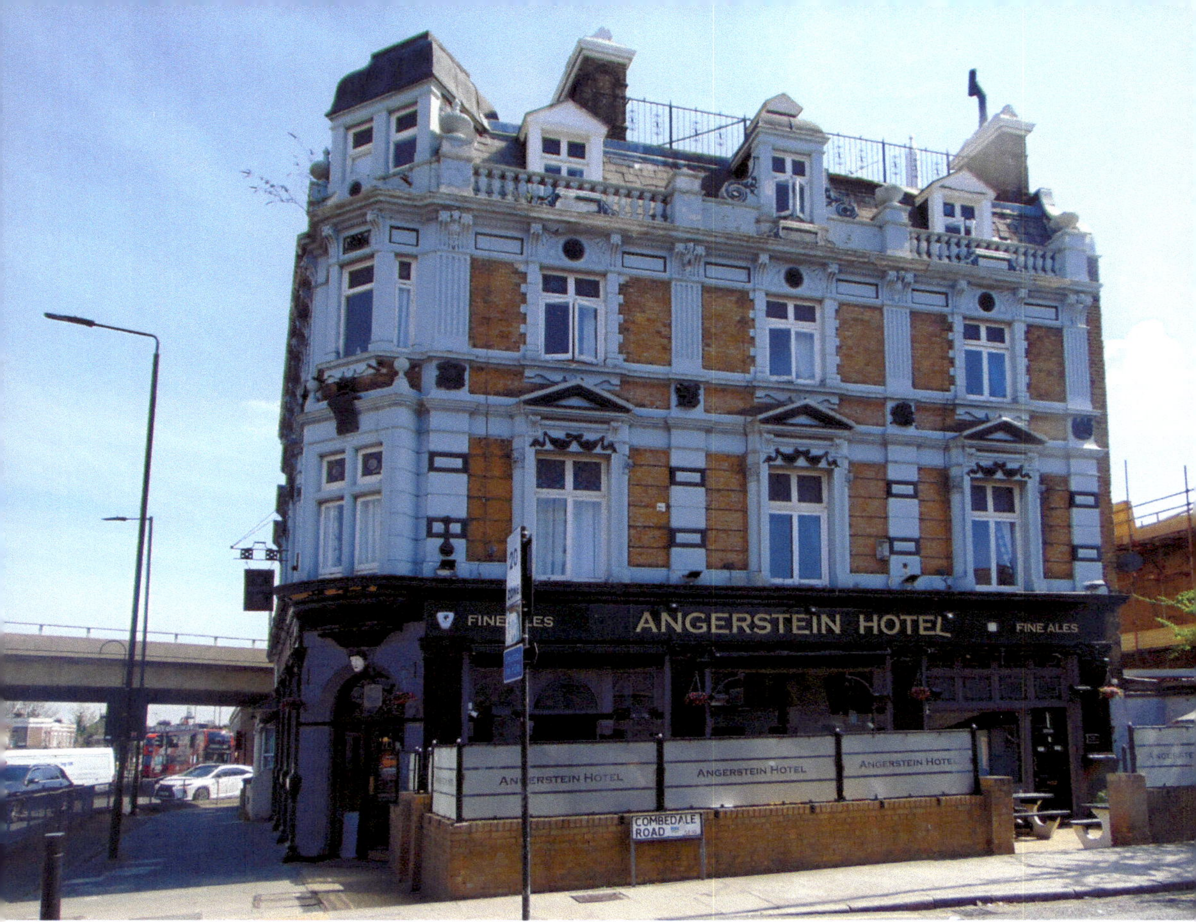

The Angerstein on the busy junction of Woolwich Road.

large U-shaped wooden-built counter with decorative etched mirrors as backdrops positioned centrally. The floors above consisted of a range of bedrooms to accommodate travellers journeying to Greenwich for pleasure as well as business, the hotel close to the former industrial area of Greenwich Marsh.

Over a period of time, the ground floor bars went through a series of refurbishments and were opened up into one large space, with the counter retained at the centre.

During the evening of 1 June 2017, a small electrical fire broke out in the office of the hotel, the smoke forcing a dozen or more pub goers to evacuate out into the street, the upstairs bedroom occupants making their escape after the fire alarm sounded. As the fire began to spread, fire crews from nearby East Greenwich, assisted by crews from Deptford and Poplar, arrived in time to put out the blaze before any serious damaged occurred.

Showing some of the old British spirit, licensee owner Sherri Mills kept the bar open to serve the regulars while repairs and decorations were carried out.

The pub's interior retains some of the features from times past, and although the large bar windows are now clear panes of glass, at the very top are the original panels of stain glass of varying patterns and colours. With several large screens positioned

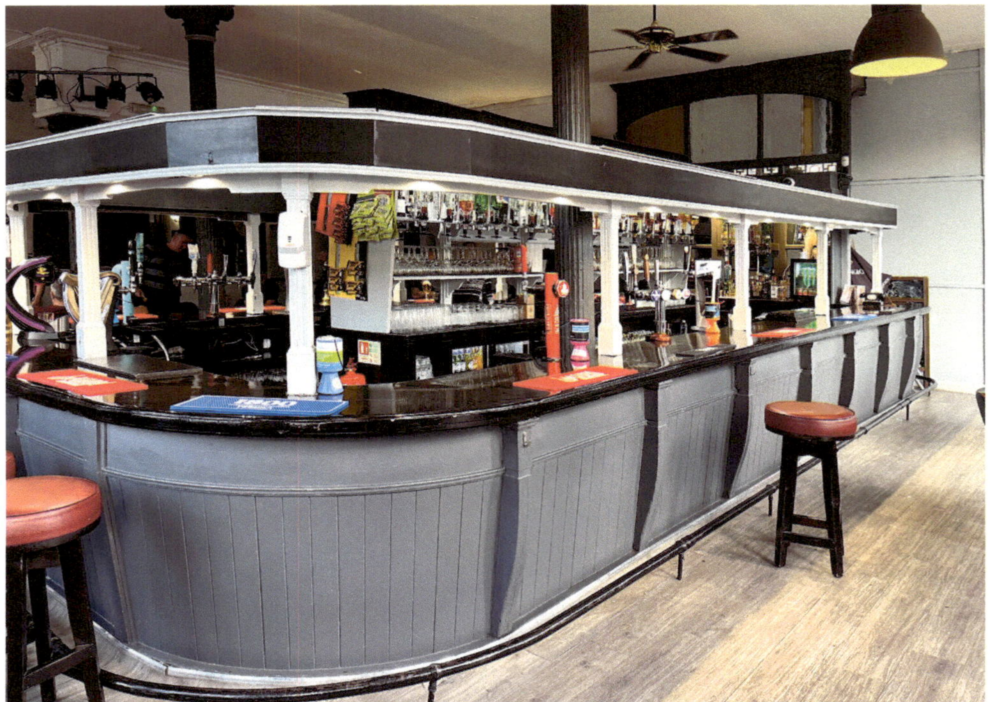

The refurbished large bar of the Angerstein Hotel.

around the bar, showing various live sports events, when Charlton Athletic football club are playing home games at The Valley, just under a mile to the east, the Angerstein Hotel has been designated as a stop-off pub for away supporters to have a beer before the match, as well as after, whatever the result.

THE GREEN GODDESS, Vanbrugh Park

Occupying a former bank, a listed building dating to the nineteenth century, Common Rioters Brewery, run by Stephen and Maryann O'Connor, opened a nano-brewery, the Green Goddess, in the refurbished property during the summer of 2022. The brewery first began trading by operating pop-up venues at the Royal Arsenal, Lesnes Abbey Farmers Market, and the grounds of Charlton House on market days.

This new nano-brewery was named Green Goddess after the Samarian goddess of beer and farming, Ninkasi, the independently run brewery taking its own name from the Plumstead Common Riots of 1876, when a military force attempted to enclose the common, a popular recreational area used by the local residents.

The ground floor of the old bank was converted into a contemporary style Belgian café/bar, with the nano-brewery located in the north end of the building, where around 500 litres of beer is intended to be brewed at a time. With up to twenty different lines of beers, plus cider and wine available, along with new and rare canned and bottled brews, the Green Goddess will also offer light bar snacks and hot drinks too.

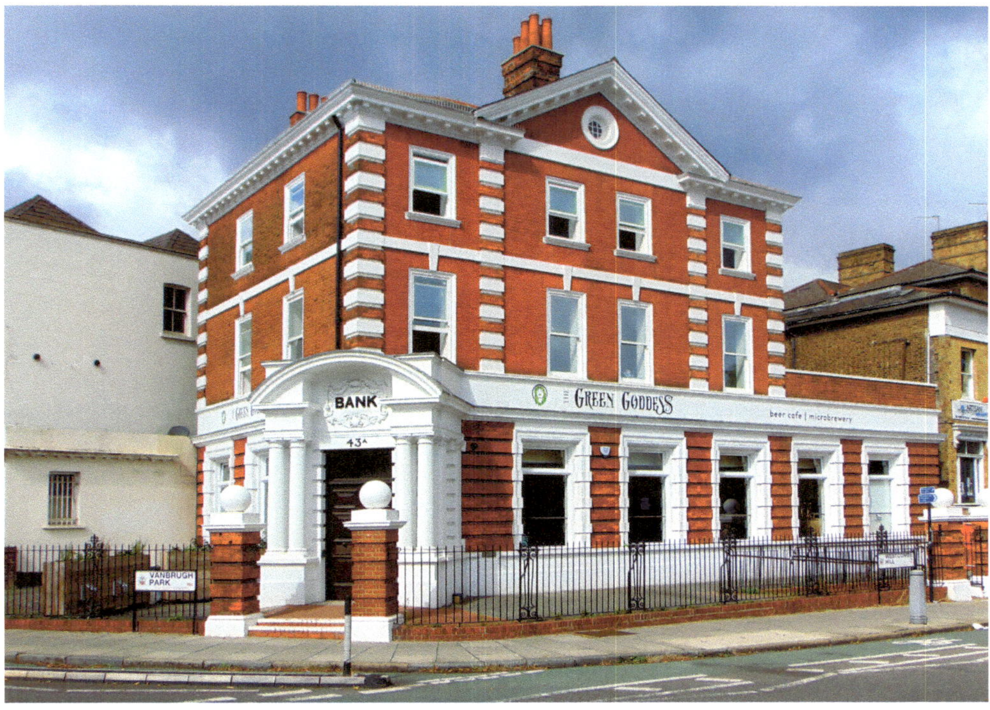

The Green Goddess – a bank of beer.

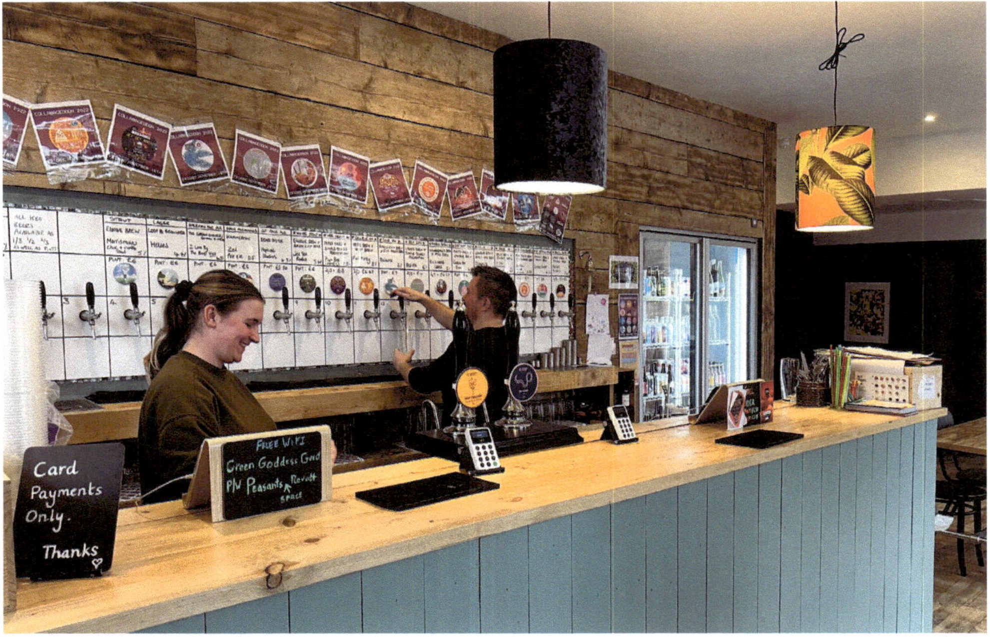

The Green Goddess nano-brewery bar, with bartender Rachel and owner Stephen.

The Green Goddess holds events throughout the year, Beer Stories, where guests are invited to join in with an entertaining evening of beer sampling, talks and conversation all about their favourite brews. The Green Goddess soon became a popular place to drink and socialise not only for existing locals, but also new residents moving into this up-and-coming area of Greenwich, on the very outskirts of Blackheath.

THE ROYAL STANDARD, Vanbrugh Park

With the Royal Borough of Greenwich's many links with kings and queens, Blackheath became a favourite place where royalty would convene to greet overseas dignitaries, and for public events and festivals. In 1400, Henry VI met the Emperor of Byzantium on the heath, and Londoners gathered there to welcome back Charles II during the Restoration in 1660, and it was on the heath where kings of England rested with their forces when venturing out on crusades to the holy land and conquests in Europe.

Blackheath, however, was also well known as a place of insurrection, from protests by marching and rioting peasants to chartists preaching revolution.

The last pub on the extremity of Greenwich parish took its name for patriotic motivations, the Royal Standard named to prove loyalty to the crown, in opposition to the recent revolutionary chartist messages coming from their mass rallies and gatherings on Blackheath in the early 1800s.

The Royal Standard – on the edge of insurrection.

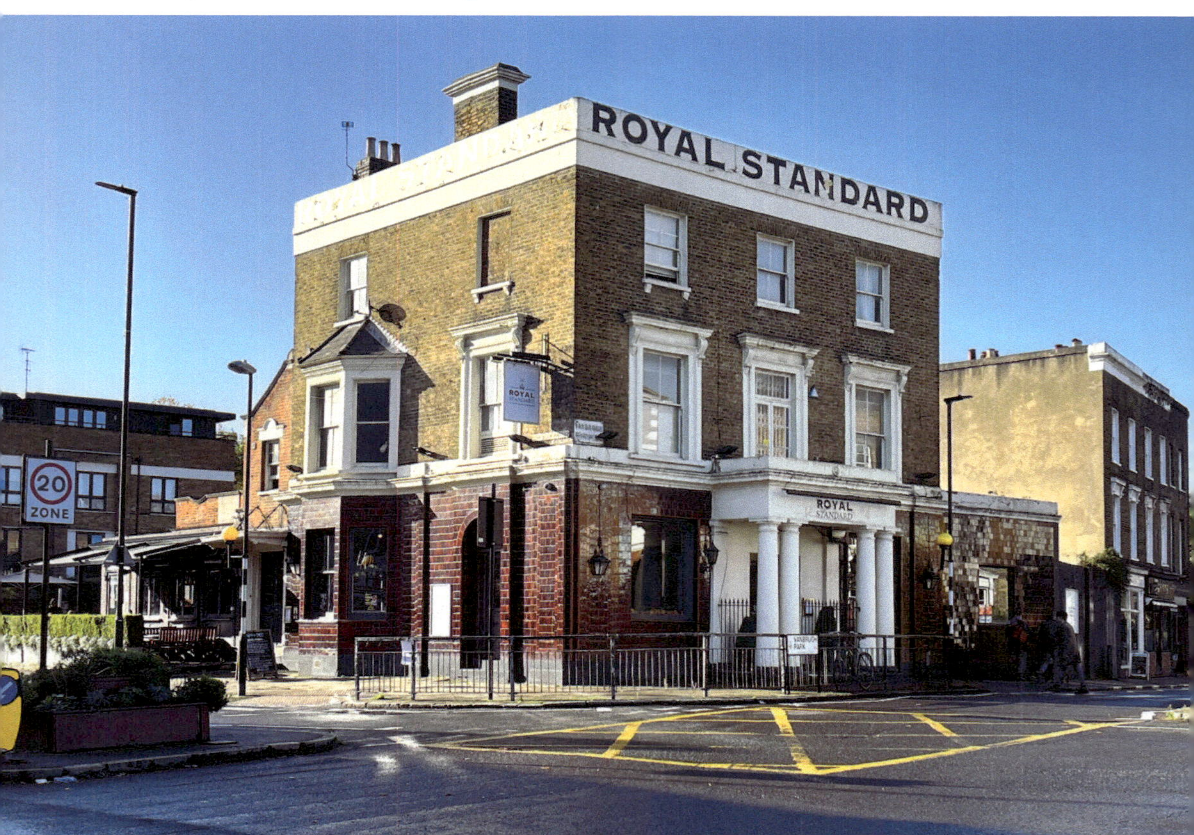

Built by William Wyn on land known as Myrtle Place, at a cost of £2,000, the Royal Standard was opened in 1848 under the management of George Edington. Around this time, as detailed on an Ordnance Survey map, surveyed in 1867, the few existing residential properties shown at the time, along with the pub, were surrounded by fields and orchards. Within fifty years, a majority of the green open spaces had disappeared, replaced by houses and shops, as well as the villas of wealthy industrialists, bankers, and merchants situated to the south of the pub towards Blackheath, an area known as St John's, the orchard trees replaced by plain trees lining the highways and byways of this newly established community.

In the 1870s, the Royal Standard was involved in a minor rebellion of its own when it joined a consortium of pubs selling sealed packs of tea in response to the unregulated competition of grocers selling beer and wine.

For sporting entertainment the Royal Standard had a bowling green, said to have been the biggest and best in Kent, and the pub also sponsored the Royal Standard Cricket Club, formed by a group of local tradesmen. By the early 1900s, the pub's name began to be used to identify this leafy green corner of Blackheath as the Royal Standard.

During the early 1970s, while in my final year of secondary school at Blackheath Bluecoat, which was a short walk to the Royal Standard, with a couple of my

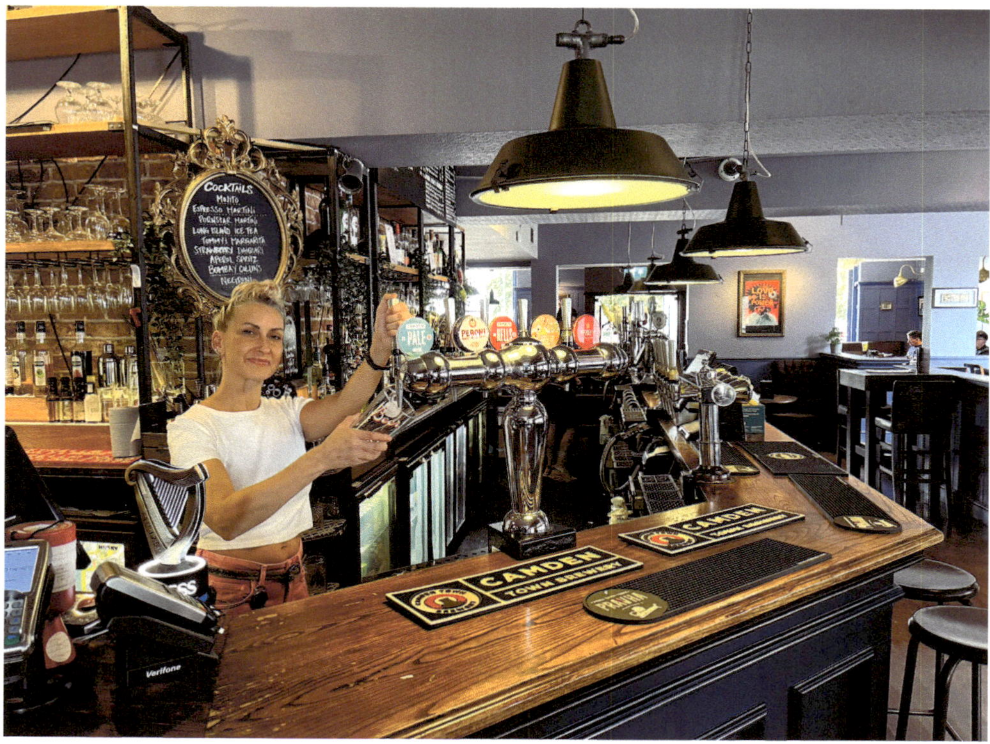

Licensee Caroline Barrett, on duty in the bar of the Royal Standard.

classmates we occasionally went to the pub during lunchtime for a pint and a sandwich. On finishing our education the Royal Standard became a popular place to go for a night out at the weekend, as one of the bars where music was played was also furnished with seated booths, each with its own telephone. From the booth you were able to make calls to people sitting at other booths, the calls made mostly to chat to members of the opposite sex – this was long before the introduction of speed dating.

As with a majority of pubs trading throughout the 1900s, the Royal Standard went through various refurbishments and much of the Victorian décor has long since gone, along with the booths and telephones. When Mark and Caroline Barrett took over the Mitchell and Butlers tied pub, around 2016, the Royal Standard was updated further, the interior now divided into two bright distinct open areas, with the bar running along the back wall between both.

There are snug alcoves and a conservatory with tables and chairs for drinking and dining, the pub offering a selection of beers and home-cooked food. The left-hand side of the pub is furnished with plush modern sofas, tables, and chairs, where quiz nights, comedy nights, live music nights and charity events take place, and at the opposite end of the pub there is a flat screen showing live sports. Outside the Royal Standard, to the rear, there is now a spacious landscaped beer garden, where the popular sport of bowls was once played.

The Future of Greenwich Pubs

In past years, most local Greenwich pub goers had their own favourite boozer, usually situated in the local community where they lived and worked, and where they would go after a day's hard graft, to converse with friends and colleagues to put the world to rights over a pint, meet up with family and friends at weekends and bank holidays, or when going for a pub crawl around Greenwich.

Once an ingrained part of British leisure time, through the late 1900s, with changing habits and lifestyles, people's attitudes towards the traditional old-time pub began to change, and many of Greenwich's pubs were required to diversify to survive.

As Greenwich emerged from the twentieth century and into the twenty-first century, many of the local pubs where we once gathered to have a drink and a chat or when meeting up to play a game of darts or bar billiards before setting off for a football match had closed their doors for good. Several Greenwich pubs were forced to close by failing to adapt to the needs of a changing society, while others fell by the wayside through excessive financial pressure placed on tenants by rent increases, and ties locking them into exclusive, but costly, stock purchase deals with the pub chain or brewers.

The recent Covid pandemic also had an adverse effect on Greenwich pubs, the loss of revenue causing financial instability, and it may be some time before sales reach pre-pandemic levels.

Pubs which survived had to become more proactive in an ever-evolving community by serving good quality meals at affordable prices and accommodating family groups, as well as capitalising on showing live sport broadcasts on large screens. During national and international festivals, anniversaries and commemorations, many pubs have engaged their customers in associated themed activities, along with hosting celebratory formal and informal gatherings and get-togethers.

Most recently, in December 2022, one of the busiest periods in a pubs calendar year leading up to the Christmas festivities, many local pubs were also celebrating the FIFA World Cup finals, their local drinkers joining in with sweepstakes and football-themed quizzes, the boost of beer sales estimated to increase by 28 per cent throughout the tournament.[4]

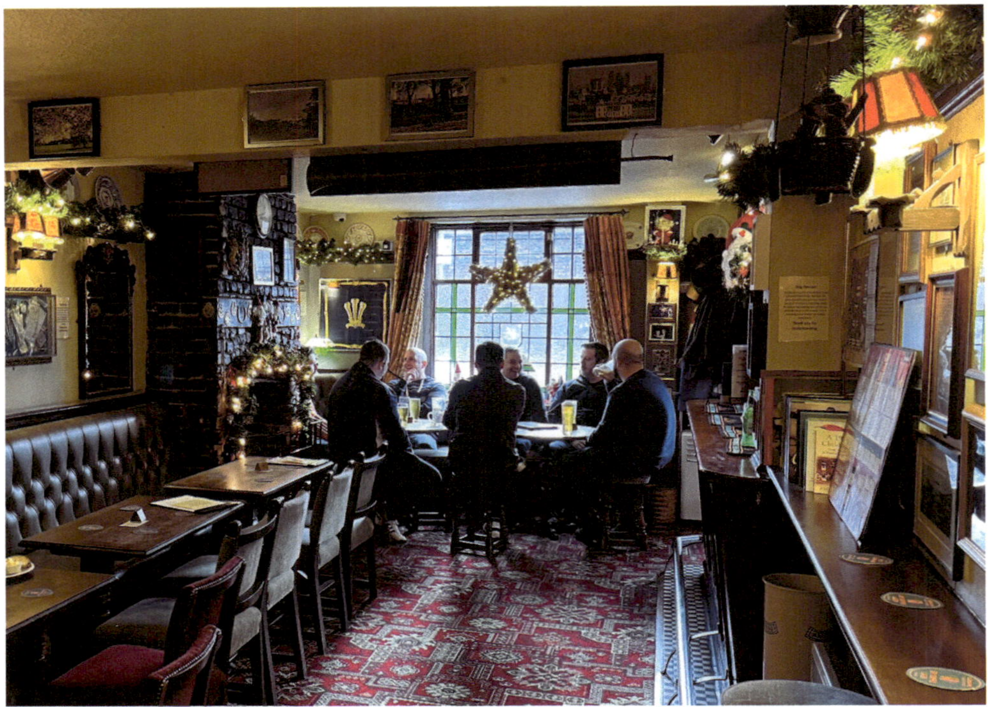

University of Greenwich former students meet up at the Plume of Feathers on the first Saturday of December 2022 for the sixteenth year in succession.

Pubs also began to utilise their location in the tourism areas of Greenwich, finding their own niche in the pub market, offering good home-cooked fayre, gastro meals or continental cuisine to visitors and tourists coming to Greenwich.

Outside of the option of food, many Greenwich pubs were required to offer customers something new and different, such as stocking a wider range of drinks and lesser-recognised beers, along with local brews, craft and cask ales, and an expansive range of wines, spirits, and cocktails, the old-time port and lemon replaced by thirst quenchers such as Aperol Spritz.

In an attempt to ensure pubs were recognised for their importance in the community, legislation introduced now gives local people the opportunity to nominate their pub an Asset of Community Value, offering pubs some protection against redevelopment, and providing communities the prospect of purchasing or leasing the pub, and then to run it for themselves.

While there have been many successes in the number of new-build pubs, microbreweries and bars opening within the old Greenwich parish boundary, pubs, old and new, will need to continue following modern trends to ensure they offer a service which encourages local people to venture across their threshold on a regular basis. Pubs can leverage good will by reminding residents, new and established, they are still part of the local community by getting involved in local events and providing space

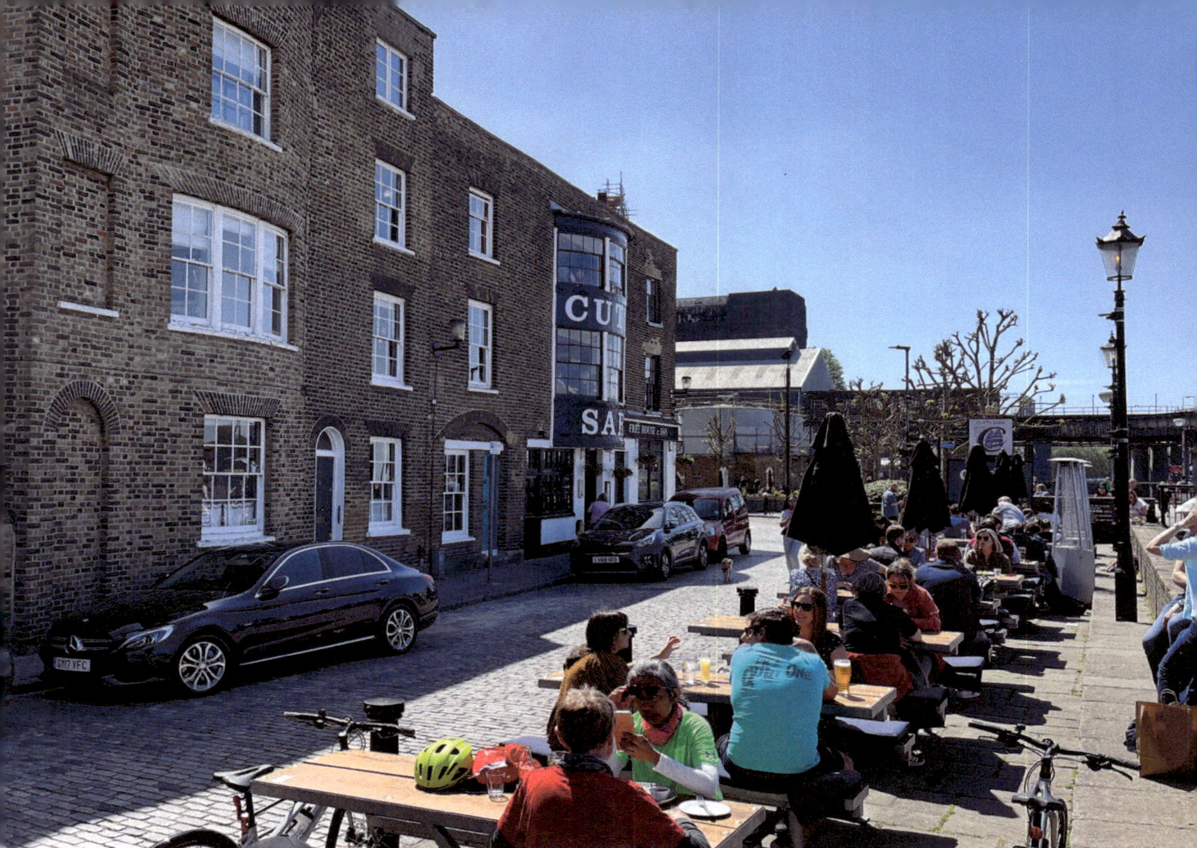

Summer's day out for a beer by the river, Cutty Sark, 2022.

for group meetings and charity fundraising, and it is paramount pub companies and chains support their individual pubs, allowing them the freedom and encouragement to engage in these important community activities.

Although the community where I lived has changed since I first began going out for a drink with my friends and relations to our local pubs, the remaining Greenwich public houses will continue to need the support from their regulars and the visitors to the riverside town, to ensure they survive and serve their local communities into the future.

Bibliography

Books

Aslet, Clive, *The Story of Greenwich* (Fourth Estate Limited, 1999)
Kelly's Directory of Kent (London, Kelly & Co., 1882)
Rhind, Neil, and Watson, Julian, *Greenwich Revealed* (Blackheath Society) Shoberl,
  William, *A Summer's Day at Greenwich* (Henry Colburn, 1840)
Strutt, Joseph, *The Sports and Pastimes of the People of England* (William Reeves,
  1803)
Weinreb, Ben, and Hibbert, Christopher, *The London Encyclopaedia* (Pan MacMillan,
  1983)

Websites

British-History Online, Dover-Kent Archives, Greenwich Industrial History Society,
Historic-UK, National Archives, Old Maps Online, Pub History Society, Victorian
Web, Vision of Britain, and the Wellcome Collection.

Notes

1. The Tied House System, Craft Beer and Brewing.
2. 'Why London's pubs are disappearing', *The Economist*, August 2017.
3. National Archives Currency Converter.
4. News, The British Beer and Pub Association, 9 December 2022.

Acknowledgements

The author and publisher would like to thank the following for their assistance in research for this publication: all the owners, licensees and managers of the pubs included in this book, British Library, Davy & Co. Limited, Greenwich Heritage Centre, Lovibonds Brewery, Meantime Brewery, National Archive, Old Royal Naval College, and the retailors at postcard fairs and antiquarian shops who have assisted in locating images and photographs. If for any reason I have not accredited people or organisations as necessary, or used copyright material without permission/ acknowledgement, I apologise for any oversight, and we will make the necessary correction at the first opportunity.

Special thanks to residents and former residents of Greenwich, who I have spent many long hours with in our local pubs over the years, for information and memories shared and recorded in this book: Alan Armstrong, Colin Barker, Geoffrey Billingsley, Andy Billingsley, Brett Cimmering, David Goggin, Dave Headley, Les Henry, Stuart Jefferies, Brian Little, Steve MacHattie, Gerry McCarthy, Maurice Oliver, Dave and Steve Overy, Jim and Paul Welch.

Images: page 9, Wellcome Collection.

About the Author

Born in Greenwich, London, David Ramzan has always had a keen interest in the history of his hometown and studied local history as an undergraduate at the University of Oxford. A self-employed graphic designer, illustrator and artist, he also worked in special educational needs and has written several historical publications and articles for magazines and periodicals, subjects which include local history, maritime and football history, piracy, smuggling and Victorian crime.